SUCCESS
PLAN FOR
LIFE

HOW TO BUILD
REAL WEALTH, DIRECTION,
AND LEGACY

CARL LENOCKER

Paperback ISBN: 979-8-9945498-0-3

Ebook ASIN: B0FWGXCDZ.

Dedication

To my wife, Erin, who inspired me to do things I didn't know I could, and to my daughters Avery and Scarlet for giving my life purpose.

TABLE OF CONTENTS

INTRODUCTION
READ THIS FIRST

If you think your starting point disqualifies you from building a great life, you and I are about to have a very honest conversation.

I didn't grow up in a place where people talked about success. I grew up in a place where people talked about *surviving the month*. Where rent was a miracle, not a guarantee.

Where you measured progress in inches, not miles.

I wasn't handed a blueprint. I didn't inherit a roadmap. I started at zero—actually, below zero—and had to dig my way out before I ever got to level ground.

So, when I tell you that where you start doesn't mean a damn thing, I need you to understand something: I'm not saying it to sound motivational. I'm saying it because I lived it.

Today, I'm in the top 1 percent of Customer Success Executives in the enterprise software world—the part of the industry where the stakes are high, the deals are massive, and the pressure will break a weak backbone in under a month.

Fortune 10 leaders and software companies pay me $400 an hour for strategic advice and much more for speaking engagements and trainings.

I've built a seven-figure net worth, many times over. I can take my family anywhere, any time.

The Rolex Sky-Dweller on my wrist isn't a flex, it's a daily reminder of how far you can travel when you refuse to stay where you began.

But here's the thing you need to know before you turn another page. None of that happened because I got lucky. It happened because I built systems. And then I built my life around those systems.

Most people try to run their lives on hope and hustle. That works… until it doesn't. Until your job changes, your energy changes, your relationships crack, your finances slip, and suddenly the wheels fall off because there was no structure underneath the grind.

When I walk into a boardroom at a Fortune 10 company, nobody cares about motivation. They care about clarity. They care about priorities. They care about execution. They care about repeatable systems that work even on the days people don't feel like working.

That's the secret nobody tells you. The same systems that run billion-dollar companies can run your life. And when you apply them consistently, everything changes. *Success Plan for Life* contains everything you need to build yourself those systems.

It's the operating system behind every major upgrade I've made: financially, professionally, physically, emotionally, and as a husband and father. It's the playbook my wife and I used to break out of our pasts, raise strong kids, build wealth, and create a life that doesn't collapse under stress.

I'm not here to impress you. I'm here to hand you the tools so you can build your own version of this life: the version that fits *you*, not me. If you've been drifting, reacting, or hoping things get better, it's time to stop.

Hope is not a plan. Motivation is not a system. Winging it is not a strategy. You deserve a life designed on purpose. *Success Plan for Life* will show you how to build it, step by step, page by page. If I can climb out of where I started, you can climb out of wherever you are now.

Turn the page.

Let's get to work.

—Carl Lenocker

P.S.

And yes, the real, unfiltered playbook for making serious money in enterprise software is in here. But trust me, it'll hit a lot harder once you've heard my story and built your own foundation to make that kind of life worth pursuing. Stick with me until the end, and you'll find a special bonus chapter that answers any remaining questions you may have.

CHAPTER 1
STARTING FROM ZERO

If I could do this, so could you.

I wasn't born into wealth and success, but it's no accident my life turned out this way.

I came into this world in 1976 in Austin, Texas, the son of a broke, forty-year-old Air Force Senior Master Sergeant on his third marriage. After twenty-two years of military service—much of it spent in Vietnam—my father had exactly *nothing* to show for it but PTSD and alimony payments. To add insult to injury, my uncle, who'd been entrusted to watch over Dad's prized 1966 Mustang during his overseas deployment, sold it and kept the money. My father didn't even have a car.

My mother was a twenty-seven-year-old British national with a kind heart, sharp wit, a can-do attitude, and incredible courage. She was living at home with her parents, a waitress in a pub by night and raising an eight-year-old son by day, when my father swept her off her feet while stationed in England. She left my half brother with my grandparents, and followed my dad to Thailand, where they lived near a US base outside Bangkok for a year in what can only be described as shabby hut-like accommodations—cold showers, geckos on the walls, and barely enough money to get by.

Their idea of a big date night, in those days, was to walk to the open-air theater on base, where they would watch films outside with other service members and their girlfriends while having a few drinks. Usually toward the end of the night, US bombers would return to base, and buzz the movie theater on their way in, to let everyone know they were back, and mess with the moviegoers. My mom said they were so close you could almost reach out and touch them, and that some airmen threw their empty beer cans in the air to try.

To underline what a grand adventure it all was, she once told me that while six months pregnant with me, she had to cross the Mekong River, alone except for a Thai girlfriend of another airman who spoke almost no English, to renew her visa in Laos.

How does one end up in a situation like that? Well, my mother had overstayed her visa and was in danger of being expelled from the country and being separated from my father. They could have bribed the Bangkok chief of police like everyone else did, but there was one problem: They didn't have any money. That would become a recurring theme in our family's story.

My dad couldn't take time off; there was a war going on, after all. The boat my mother boarded was barely seaworthy, overloaded with people, chickens, and pigs. Tires hung from its sides. Distant gunfire echoed up the river. As the boat crawled across the brown current, she became certain that if it didn't sink, they'd all end up in the hands of the Communists.

Despite her terror, she lived to tell the tale. The border agent who stamped her passport on the Laotian side took one look at her—alone, pregnant, without luggage—and said, "You don't belong here. You go back to England soon," in a tone that made her blood run cold.

A few months later, at eight months pregnant, my dad used his last dime to buy her a plane ticket to San Francisco, where they'd reunite and start their life together. He gave her his final twenty bucks and promised to meet her in two days. What could possibly go wrong, you might ask?

Two days turned into five.

She'd heard stories of soldiers who'd vanished after promises of marriage and a new life, and she was beginning to lose faith.

In classic form, after talking the hotel front desk into giving her a room on her word that her husband would arrive soon and pay the bill (my parents were not yet married), she ran out of money on her first day in San Francisco and survived the coming days only on extra chocolates begged from hotel maids during service. When my father finally arrived, she was hours from going to the British Consulate to request help getting home. Instead, they boarded a Greyhound bus together to Austin, to kick off their new life.

Along the way, my father cashed a post-dated twenty-dollar check with help from a kind officer making the same trip. Upon arrival in Austin, he bought snacks, cigarettes, and told a taxi driver, "If you want a tip, you better let us out when the meter hits five dollars." The driver turned off the meter and drove them the rest of the way for free.

My parents took up residency in the manager's tiny quarters behind a roach-infested motel in Del Valle called The Country Cottages. The owner, Colonel Parker, an old Air Force connection, agreed to let my parents manage the place as a favor to my dad, more for free rent than profit.

A short time later, I was born in St. David's Hospital. My dad had to sell back a month of military vacation time to pay the bill. He also had to confess to my mother that he was still technically married to his second wife, which meant they couldn't officially wed until the divorce was final, which was a few months after I arrived.

Fitting, I guess. My first act on this Earth was to wipe out what little our family had, completely. How else could I claim later in life that I literally came from nothing?

When I came home from the hospital, our possessions included three plastic plates, three forks, and a garage-sale dinner table with a trick leg that would fall off unless someone held it in place while everyone else sat down.

There wasn't much to work with, but somehow, they were happy. There was optimism, that sense that if we could just catch a break, things would finally turn a corner for the Lenockers.

We had that same table until I was sixteen.

The Millionaires Next Door

This year, my wife and I will generate over a half million dollars—the most we've ever made. We both come from incredibly modest beginnings. Neither of us ever thought we'd get here.

Our net worth is compounding rapidly, and we're on track to retire comfortably, on our own terms, with a freedom most people never taste. With freedom my parents never got to experience.

We're not private-jet rich. We don't even drive new cars. We're millionaires-next-door rich.

And looking back on where we started, that's more than enough.

It's a liberating thing when you realize you will have enough—when work becomes more of a choice instead of a necessity. Your mind opens. Life expands. You finally start living.

Even better, we're happy and healthy. Our twin daughters just graduated college—only the second generation in our family to earn degrees, and they did it on time in four years. My mom always said you can't fake raising good kids, and we couldn't be prouder of ours.

They're both fully independent, working in sales, and living near the beach, just as they'd plotted in their own success plans.

We've invested in their futures, and now we get to watch those investments pay off.

The Plan Behind It All

It took a lot to get here.

Years of careful planning. Reading. Reflection. Relationship-building. Therapy. Long nights. Tough conversations. More failures than I can count.

But we mapped our goals, built a plan, and faced the future with intention. We overcame our childhoods, not by luck, but by design.

This book is about how you can do the same.

Whether your goals are financial freedom, better health, stronger relationships, or simply taking control of your time, the frameworks ahead will help you build a success plan for life.

I'm not here to sell you a fantasy.

I'm here to show you how to build your life with the same structure, strategy, and clarity that build great companies while helping you avoid the land mines I stepped on along the way.

As I sit here today, with a career I love, a family I adore, and a sense of peace I once thought I'd never find, I know none of it was luck. Every win came from a plan.

And that plan didn't start in a spreadsheet or a fancy office.

It started in the cab of a rusty Freightliner.

In the rubble of failed relationships.

And, apparently, in a dive bar run by a WWII vet who taught me generosity before I could even spell it.

That's where *Success Plan for Life* was born.

STOP AND REFLECT

Begin reflecting on the future life you envision for yourself. I'll ask you to get specific in later chapters, but this is a good time to begin thinking about it from a high level. Can you see it clearly, or is your vision clouded by aspects of your life, or challenges you are facing?

Looking back now, it's easy to see how those early years shaped everything that came after: the way I handled pressure, the way I saw money, the way I worked, the way I loved, the way I fought for stability like it was oxygen.

At the time, I didn't realize any of that. Most of us don't. We grow up, put our heads down, and move forward as fast as we can, trying to outrun the parts of our story that hurt... or the parts we'd rather forget.

But here's the truth I didn't learn until much later:

Your past doesn't stay in the past. It follows you. Quietly. Patiently. In your habits, your fears, your relationships, your ambition, your avoidance, your reactions.

You can't build a powerful future until you understand the engine that's been quietly steering your life this whole time.

My story is just one version of starting from zero. Yours will look different with different places, different people, different scars, different patterns. But the impact is the same.

If you want to build a life worth living, you've got to understand the one you came from.

The next chapter will help you do that. Not to relive anything. Not to get stuck back there.

But to finally see the forces that shaped you, so you can choose what comes next with clarity and intention.

Carl Lenocker

Because going forward always starts with looking back.

CHAPTER 2
GO BACK TO THE BEGINNING, SO YOU CAN MOVE FORWARD

Because until you own your origin story, it owns you.

Most people go through life trying to outrun the past. They don't look back. They don't reflect. They don't ask the harder questions. They just keep moving, hoping momentum will save them from themselves.

But here's the truth most of us spend decades avoiding: You can't outrun what shaped you.

But you *can* understand it. And once you understand it, you can change everything that comes next.

Your origin story isn't just a memory. It's the hidden operating system underneath your entire adult life. It's the reason certain things come easily to you... and why other things keep breaking at the same fault line, again and again.

You don't just inherit eye color. You inherit patterns. Stories. Silence. Expectations. Wounds. Survival tactics. Beliefs about money, love, success, conflict, and worth.

And unless you take the time to actually look at where you came from, those patterns will quietly run your life on autopilot.

Your Past Isn't the Problem, the Unexamined Past Is

The point of this chapter isn't to relive old pain.

It's to understand the map you've been using without realizing you're still holding it.

Your childhood shaped the way you respond under stress. It shaped the way you communicate, how you deal with conflict, what you avoid, what you chase, and what you fear losing most.

It shaped your ambition. Your insecurity. Your urgency. Your patience. Your financial instincts. Your tolerance for chaos. Your definition of "normal."

But here's the biggie: Your origin story is not a life sentence. It's a starting point.

A powerful one, if you're willing to look at it honestly.

Because once you understand the forces that built you, you're finally free to decide which ones get to follow you into the life you're building next.

Some Patterns Need to End With You.

Every family has patterns that run for generations like underground wiring. Some give strength. Some give resilience. Some give warmth, loyalty, humor, resourcefulness, grit.

And some give dysfunction. Scarcity. Anger. Avoidance. Addiction. Silence. Shame. Fear disguised as practicality. Chaos disguised as passion. Control disguised as love. Workaholism disguised as responsibility.

If you look closely enough, you'll see exactly which patterns were handed to you and which ones are begging to stop with you.

This isn't about blaming anyone. It's about finally naming what's been shaping you in the shadows. Because once you name it, you can change it.

Why You Feel Stuck (Even When You're Working Hard)

Most people think they're not successful yet because they're lazy, undisciplined, unorganized, or unlucky. But the truth is often simpler and deeper: You're fighting patterns you don't even know you're carrying.

If you grew up around:

- Chaos → you now normalize drama or create it.
- Silence → you don't ask for help or speak your needs.
- Criticism → you chase perfection or hide your potential.
- Scarcity → you fear risk, success, or spending money.
- Burnout → you work yourself into the ground to feel worthy.
- Instability → you cling too hard or detach too quickly.
- Uncertainty → you never trust calm.
- "Just enough" → you think big goals don't belong to you.

These patterns create invisible ceilings. They sabotage your momentum. They drain your energy. They complicate your relationships. They distort your beliefs about what's possible.

You're not broken. You're repeating. And repeating isn't destiny; it's just habit.

Going Back Is the Way Forward

This is why the early part of your Success Plan for Life requires one brave move: Look backward. Not to live there—but to understand who you had to become to survive there.

Because survival-mode behaviors don't build future success. They build exhaustion, resentment, overachievement, underachievement, and fear-driven decisions.

You don't have to keep carrying all that. Going back gives you a chance to set it down.

Once you understand your origin story, you can choose the parts you want to keep and the parts you're ready to release.

That's the moment everything opens up. That's when the future stops feeling heavy. That's when the past stops pulling you under. That's when you finally step into adulthood as the author, not the inheritance.

Going back isn't weakness. It's strategy. It's clarity. It's the doorway to a life you design on purpose.

STOP AND REFLECT

Take your time with these. Write the answers. Say them out loud. Let them unravel truth you've swallowed for years.

1. What was the emotional climate of your home growing up? How did people communicate? What was safe? What wasn't?

2. What patterns—good or bad—show up in your family across generations?

3. What did you learn about money as a child? How is that still affecting you today?

4. When you feel threatened or stressed, how do you react? Where did you learn that response?

5. Which parts of your upbringing made you strong? Which parts made you guarded?

6. What events or circumstances did you have to survive? What did you have to become to make it through?

7. Which of your current habits or struggles make perfect sense once you look backward?

8. What patterns need to continue through you? Which ones need to end with you?

9. What version of yourself did childhood create? What version do you want to build now?

Understanding your origin story is powerful... but it's often not complete until you look at the people who shaped it, especially the ones who left the deepest mark.

For me, that journey led me back to my father—his life, his struggles, his choices—and, ultimately, his death became one of the most defining moments of my adulthood.

Sometimes moving forward requires making peace with the people who came before you—even when the goodbye isn't the one you hoped for.

Turn the page. Let me tell you about mine.

CHAPTER 3
SAYING GOODBYE

Because closure begins the moment we choose to show up.

When the call came, I knew.

My father's time was near.

At seventy-nine, after a brutal hemorrhagic stroke had stripped him of his independence and mental clarity, he was confined to his bed, at home, in the Nevada desert, staring out at the birds he used to feed. Once a decorated military man and long-haul trucker who could cross the country without a map—a man who knew every bartender from coast to coast—he was now a shell of himself.

It wasn't for lack of fight. When the stroke hit that January, we went into almost immediate action. We found the best doctors, the best rehab facility in Las Vegas, and we were all full of optimism.

Just months earlier, he'd been mountain biking fifteen miles a day in the desert heat, climbing unpaved hills near my parents' home. Surely a man that strong could recover, or so we thought. Seventy-eight wasn't even considered that old anymore.

But the damage was too deep. The stroke left him largely paralyzed on his left side, prone to confusion with only brief flashes of the sharp mind we knew. The man who'd done *The New York Times* crossword every morning for fifty years now stared blankly at the grid.

The Call

Nearly a year after the stroke, he called one afternoon.

"Hey buddy," he said with a strange calm. "I'm just calling to say goodbye."

He spoke with urgency—like he knew this moment of clarity wouldn't last.

"What are you talking about, Dad? You're not going anywhere," I said, trying to sound steady.

"It's just my time, it just is," he replied quietly. "If it wouldn't be too much trouble, I'd like to see you, before I go."

My mother took the phone and explained that his demeanor had changed—that he'd started dreaming of a train coming for him, his long-departed mother on board. He said he had his ticket and suitcase ready, waiting on a platform. But his train seemed delayed.

The Hard Beginning

To say my dad had a rough start would be an understatement.

In 1939, at four years old, he found his twenty-two-year-old mother lifeless on the bathroom floor. Doctors said she'd died from cardiac arrest—a weak heart scarred from childhood scarlet fever.

It was the Great Depression. His father had left two years earlier to find work on fishing boats in Alaska and never returned. My dad took his two-year-old sister by the hand and led her next door to ask for help.

They stayed briefly with grandparents, but when it became clear the family couldn't afford two more mouths to feed, the children were put up for adoption.

Both were taken in by nearby farmers who couldn't have kids of their own. My dad never shared many details—just that life on that farm was hard. Up at 4:30 a.m. to milk cows. Exhausted at school. Beaten down but determined, he'd collect bottles on the county road that bordered theirs to return for deposits, as his first side-hustle.

One summer in his teens, while cutting wood, a log crushed his adoptive father's leg, leaving my dad to run the entire farm alone for months. When the leg finally healed, the old man stepped out onto the front porch, looked around and didn't say *Thank You*, but instead only, "Those cows look skinny."

That was the last straw.

At seventeen, my dad lied about his age and joined the Army, escaping to Germany as part of the "elite" Berlin Brigade. His adopted mother, in tears, only figured out why as his train pulled away from the platform.

The Soldier Years

He loved the camaraderie and the adventure. By day, he served his country. By night, he ran a backroom blackjack game and sold black-market cigarettes to the locals. When his pay occasionally disappeared in poker losses, he spent his days reading nearly every book in the library, he'd later recount proudly.

That hunger to learn became his lifelong habit.

He used to joke that the only thing "elite" about the Berlin Brigade was that they'd be the first to die if the Russians crossed the border. They stored their beer on their barracks window ledges, because the freezing temps outside kept it ice cold and within easy reach. Their ammunition was stored miles away—sacrificial lambs by design.

After two years in the Army, he enlisted in the Air Force for twenty more. It took him around the world: Germany, Japan, Johnston Atoll, Vietnam, Thailand, England, and everywhere in between.

By the time he retired, he'd collected three marriages, three kids, and more stories than regrets—though there were plenty of both.

The Long Goodbye

When I arrived in Nevada, he was a shadow of the man I remembered.

I sat beside his bed and watched him sleep. Sometimes for hours.

Mom told me he'd been sleeping more and more—sometimes forty-eight hours at a stretch—waking to talk about trains or long-gone faces he swore were standing in the corner.

On the second day, she held off his morphine until I arrived. When I walked in, he looked more alert than anyone had seen him in weeks.

He smiled and reached for his wallet, on the nightstand.

"Check this out," he said, pulling out his American Express card. "Member Since: 1953. What do you think of that?"

I smiled. "That's a long time, Dad."

That green card he got back in 1953 had bailed us out of more than one jam growing up. I couldn't help but laugh. Of course this was what he wanted to talk about—the last conversation we'd ever have.

From across the room, Mom called, "What are you showing him?"

"I'm giving the boy the deed to the farm," he said with a chuckle.

I'm not sure if he believed it or was just being funny.

A Private Moment

Mom rolled out of the room in her wheelchair, leaving us alone. She had been dealing with her own struggles with bad health, depression, and lifelong addiction that were finally catching up with her. As if this situation couldn't be sadder, she could no longer walk more than a few steps without falling over.

Dad leaned close. "Are you going to be okay?" he whispered.

He was talking about more than his death. My mother had lawyers coming the next day to change the will, to write me out completely. Our relationship had been broken for years—too much pain, too much pride. She wouldn't get the help she needed, and I was done appeasing her. This was her last attempt at hurting me.

I nodded. "Yeah, Dad. Don't worry; I'll be fine."

Then I looked around to make sure Mom was gone, leaned close to his ear, and whispered, "I'm a millionaire."

His eyes widened. For a second, confusion, then understanding.

"You are?" he whispered back in near disbelief, but then a slow smile spread across his face. "Of course you are. I knew you would do it."

The Final Conversation

A winter storm was coming, and I had to start back to Colorado. I hugged him tight, tears welling up.

The irony was not lost on me that I had to leave to beat a storm, as that was usually his line, when I was growing up.

He patted my back with his one good hand. Always steady. Always comforting.

"Are you afraid to die?" I asked quietly.

"No," he said. "I'm ready."

The man who'd protected me my whole life was still doing it— even now.

"When the train comes," I told him, "you get on it, okay?"

"Okay," he nodded, still patting my back.

"I love you, Dad," I said.

He kept patting. "Okay."

He couldn't say it back. His life had been too hard. Something inside him had broken long ago—the part that could say those words aloud. I understood.

And I promised myself that my daughters would never have to excuse me for the same.

Before I left, he gave me his final instructions:

"Take my guns and keep them in the family."

"Take care of those girls. Make sure they finish college."

"If you need me, I'll be at that spot we picked out, out in the desert under the Joshua tree."

I nodded, turned, and walked out of the room.

That was the last time I saw my father alive.

STOP AND REFLECT

When the people who shaped you are gone, what part of them will live on through the way you lead, love, or show up for others?

And are you living in a way that would make them proud today?

When my father died, I had just made my first million, but that didn't make the loss any lighter. What hit me hardest wasn't money. It was the shift.

Suddenly, every bit of pressure he carried for decades was on my shoulders.

I became the head of the family overnight, and losing the one man I could always call rattled me more than I understood at the time.

Grief changes you. Responsibility changes you faster. And in the middle of all of it, I threw myself deeper into the one arena that could reshape my family's future: my career. The role that would become my identity, my leverage, and the foundation of everything I built next.

But back then, even I didn't really know what to make of it. Because honestly?

Everyone kept asking me, What the hell *is* a Customer Success Manager?

Now I'm finally ready to answer that question.

CHAPTER 4
WHAT THE HELL IS A CUSTOMER SUCCESS MANAGER?

And why doing it well gave me the blueprint for building an intentional life.

A lot of people who pick up this book probably have the same question: "What exactly is a Customer Success Manager?"

It's fair; especially since the role barely existed ten years ago. Hell, it barely exists now.

If you follow Big Tech news, you've seen it: Every few months another major software company lays off its entire Customer Success Department. Usually because of bad leadership, unclear value, or simply a lack of people who have "it."

And what is *it*?

Let's rewind a bit.

The Wild West of Tech

Twenty-five years ago, the tech industry felt like an open frontier.

I started on the help desk—in the trenches of tech support—where I discovered something important: I was good with people. Even angry, frustrated people. *Especially* them.

Then one day my job got offshored to India. Just like that, I had to pivot fast. If you weren't nimble, you were toast.

I bounced around for a few years—technical roles, management, back to technical again—until I realized where to find the real opportunity: working for a software vendor.

They were selling big-time solutions to big-time problems, with profit margins that made Wall Street get fired up. Friends were getting rich at rates I hadn't seen since the dot-com boom, and I wanted in. Companies offered remote work for those who wanted it, but if they chose to come in, there were perks like free beer in the break room.

But the trick was carving out your own role—building a business case for why companies should pay you handsomely to do what you do best. It took me a while to figure that out.

Anything that could be easily explained or automated was out.

I wanted to do the work no one could quite define—the kind that makes you indispensable.

So, What Exactly Is a CSM?

Even today, ask ten people what Customer Success is, and you'll get twelve answers.

We're not salespeople, though we often own expansion and renewals.

We're not support, though we get dragged into technical issues constantly.

We're not product, though we push for features and adoption.

We're not marketing, though we spend half our time telling stories that inspire clients to take action.

At its core, Customer Success is about helping clients not just *use* a product but get measurable, lasting value from it.

We're the wizards who walk between raindrops, the ones who manage everything that happens after the sale, and then some.

You bought something that doesn't do what was promised? That's on me.

Your boss doesn't recognize your results? Let's fix that.

Your project's losing momentum? I'll rally the team.

A competitor is undercutting us on price? I'll show you why that move could cost you your job.

And we're just getting started.

A CSM is part consultant, part program manager, part therapist, part world traveler, part sommelier, part motivational speaker, part casino host.

There have been days when I'm bussing tables, and running drinks from the bar, because the restaurant we're meeting at is short staffed; I literally try to own every aspect of the customer experience I can.

And when it's done right, it's one of the most strategic roles in the business world.

It forces you to think like an owner, plan like a general, and serve like a trusted adviser.

CSMs live in game-theory mode twenty-four-seven—always pondering, How do I outthink the person in front of me? That person could be your boss, your client, their boss, the hotel front desk clerk who is trying to stick you in a shitty room, or the narcissistic egomaniacal sales rep you might be attached to who is blocking you from engaging with his account, because he fears you're going to blow the big deal he's been working on for months.

But if done right, you become the heartbeat between the client's outcomes and your company's revenue. You own relationships with key stakeholders that will pay off handsomely over time. Your boss recognizes your contribution and rewards you generously. You end up in the quiet room on a high floor, far away from the elevator.

It's Not About Churn, It's About Outcomes

Most people think CSMs exist to make sure clients don't leave. And that's part of it.

But if you're only focused on retention, you're already too late.

Any account that isn't expanding is dying.

The moment a client signs, the clock starts ticking, and so does the risk of losing them.

Great CSMs think in roadmaps, not renewals.

They define success before the contract ink dries. They build pro-active plans to drive results, not reactions.

In my role, I've helped some of the world's largest companies navigate the following:

- $100M+ digital transformation projects
- Global software rollouts
- Vendor transitions involving thousands of users
- Executive-level strategies tied directly to financial outcomes

I wasn't just delivering software.

I was delivering success.

And somewhere along the way, I realized that the same mindset that made me great at Customer Success could make me great at life.

How CSM Thinking Built My Life

At some point, it clicked.

If I could build quarterly success plans for Fortune 10 companies, why wasn't I doing the same thing for myself?

So, I started running my life the same way I ran my accounts:

- Clear Goals
- Defined Metrics
- Tactical Execution
- Regular Reviews
- Stakeholder Alignment (yes—even with my wife and kids)

That framework—born out of survival in a high-pressure career—became my secret weapon.

It gave me focus, structure, and confidence. I wasn't just reacting to life anymore. I was leading it.

My Personal Brand of Customer Success

Over the years, I've built my own brand of CSM'ing—the version that felt true to me:

Radical Ownership: If it goes wrong, I own it. Even if I didn't cause it. That mindset builds unshakable trust.

Executive-Level Clarity: I talk to VPs and CEOs the same way I talk to my kids: simply, clearly, and with the end in mind.

Outcomes Over Optics: I don't care about dashboards. I care about impact. Did we help the client win or not?

People First, Always: Behind every logo is a human being. Every sale was made to a person. Relationships will always matter most to me.

This philosophy didn't just make me successful at work. It made me successful in life.

Because life, like business, is full of competing priorities, emotional stakeholders, and finite resources. The same playbook applies.

Why This Book Exists

I wrote this book because I believe the mindset and methods that make great CSMs can help anyone:

- Create goals that actually matter
- Build systems that last
- Align the people in their life
- Measure progress in ways that motivate, not drain

You don't need to work in tech to apply these ideas. You just need to want more from your life and be willing to plan for it.

If you can learn to run your life the way I've learned to run a $50M client portfolio, you'll be unstoppable.

What systems from your work, training, or early experiences could you apply to your personal life?

How might your "professional brain" help you design a better, more intentional life outside of work?

When I first stepped into Customer Success, I didn't have a playbook. Hell, nobody did. The role was still half-mythical, half-made-up, and everyone I asked gave me a different definition.

So, I did the only thing I knew how to do: I showed up, figured it out as I went, and tried not to let anyone realize how clueless I felt in the beginning.

But here's the thing most people don't tell you about this job: You don't learn Customer Success in a conference room. You learn it *out there*.

In airports.

In rental cars.

In meeting rooms where nobody knows your name yet.

And on the road, sitting across from customers who can smell fear, incompetence, or bullshit from a mile away. My real education didn't start with training. It started the moment I boarded my first flight as a CSM… and stepped into the world I would eventually conquer.

Alright.

Let's hit the road.

CHAPTER 5
MY FIRST TIME ON THE ROAD; WELCOME TO CUSTOMER SUCCESS!

Because no great story ever started out with, "So we were sitting in a conference room."

I was in my early thirties and seriously doubting some of my life choices that morning. I figured I'd be looking for another job by the next day, but little did I know, I was built for this world.

The receipts were still warm from my pocket, like battlefield shrapnel, and I had a sinking feeling they were about to tell me how stupid last night really was.

Six hundred dollars?

Six hundred and fifty fucking dollars?

I sat in the back of the cab to the Victoria airport, suit crumpled, tie twisted, shoes still on from the night before, head pounding like a drumline, mouth as dry as a bone.

I called my boss.

"Mike, I think I screwed up," I rasped.

"What do you mean, Carl?"

"Well… I think I spent too much money last night. The client didn't want to go home, and I think I'm in big trouble. I don't know what happened, but I've got $650 worth of receipts here."

There was silence. Then laughter—huge, belly-deep laughter.

"Mike, did you hear all that? I'm in a panic over here, man," I said, hoping he'd understand the gravity.

"Dammit, Carl," he chuckled, "you had a client who wanted to spend time with you, and you guys formed a fast friendship over some food and drink? And you think you're in trouble? Why don't you call me when you have a real problem."

Click. Call over. He hung up on me.

He'd end up promoting me a few months down the road.

Maybe I Should've Seen It Coming

Maybe I shouldn't have been so shocked. Truth is, I've always done some of my best work in bars.

When it came time for me to start walking and talking, my first word wasn't Mommy or Daddy like other kids.

It was "Leo."

You see, the small motel where we lived shared a parking lot with a little dive bar called The C&W, owned and tended by a kindly WWII vet named Leo Phelps.

Leo had once stormed the beaches of Normandy. Now he was happily retired—pouring beers, lighting cigarettes, and holding court like a small-town philosopher.

And that bar? That was my daycare.

I spent my earliest years in the C&W—a multipurpose space that doubled as our family dining room, birthday venue, and community hall. When I'd go missing from the motel as a two-year-old, my parents always knew where to look.

There I'd be, perched on a barstool next to Leo, eating a pickle while he filled my baby bottle with Dr. Pepper.

And if that's not the most Texas thing you've ever heard, I don't know what is.

One time, I wandered behind the counter and grabbed a bag of chips. A customer barked, "Hey, why doesn't that kid have to pay?"

Without missing a beat, Leo said, "That kid doesn't have to pay for anything in here. Didn't you see his name on the bar?"

Sure enough, he pointed to where my initials, C for Carl, D for David were spelled out in pennies, sealed forever under thick acrylic. I was sewn into the fabric of that place, a real made man.

You see, when my parents brought me home from the hospital and told the patrons at the C&W that my name was Carl, they thought it was ridiculous. "You can't call a baby Carl!" one of them cried out in disappointment.

It so happened that several were chipping in their labor on refinishing the bar at that very moment, and once those pennies were laid down, from that day forward all my family and close friends called me CD.

As the unofficial mascot for the bar, I took it upon myself to greet customers and get to know everyone who came and went from that little hole in the wall. I considered them all my friends, from the blue-collar workers who came in after 5 p.m. to hoist a pint on their way home, to the hardcore alcoholics who showed up before noon; I had love in my heart for all of them.

So yeah, I guess it makes sense that decades later, I'd find myself closing million-dollar deals in steakhouses and making lifelong connections in backrooms and bars. I was trained early. My first mentors just happened to serve Lone Star beer instead of management theory, but there were lessons learned nonetheless.

You have to have love in your heart for everybody, if you want to win in this world.

Now where was I, on what happened that night in Victoria, BC?

Flashback #1

A pint glass slams onto a brewpub table. Someone shouts, "One more round!" I nod like it's a legally binding agreement.

Flashback #2

The steak knife cuts clean through a ribeye at the Cactus Club. My wine glass is being refilled expertly by their famously beautiful wait staff.

Flashback #3

We're in another bar—maybe the third or the fifth—and I'm laughing at a joke I don't remember hearing. There's a live singer, from whom I am purchasing a CD, and all the Canadians think it's hilarious that I don't know the conversion rate as I overpay with cash.

Flashback #4

The sound of credit card receipts tearing from the register, a hand passing me another slip to sign. One of my clients is asleep, head down on the bar, with a full martini glass in his iron fist.

Flashback #5

One of my clients is being tossed into the alley, by security, after puking in the middle of the bar. Another client chases after, while yelling "No man left behind!" then helps him hail a taxi.

The day before had been pristine: my first trip in the field as a Customer Success Manager. My first time on the road in this business.

I'd flown to Victoria, BC, dressed like I belonged on a business magazine cover, eager to meet the client. The meeting at their office was productive, friendly—the kind of professional rapport that makes you think, *I'm going to crush this role.*

When 5 p.m. rolled around, someone floated the idea of grabbing a beer at a brewpub nearby. Perfectly reasonable.

Two beers later, the "quick drink" evolved into dinner: big, beautiful steak dinners with bottles of wine, poured by beautiful waitresses. From there, it was as if the city itself conspired to make sure we didn't go home: pub after pub, toast after toast, laughter echoing off the rain-soaked cobblestones of downtown Victoria.

The last thing I remember clearly was thinking, *This is great. I'm bonding with the client.*

The next thing I knew, my alarm was screaming at 6 a.m., and I was laid out fully dressed on the hotel bed like I'd been staged by a crime scene investigator.

That was my introduction to Customer Success—equal parts relationship-building, panic, and the kind of stories that only make sense when told years later over another drink.

To truly know me is to wine and dine with me. I may not have known it then, but in the years since, I've built quite a reputation for being the best at it.

Why are relationships that start like this usually the ones that last forever? I'm still trying to figure that out fifteen years later.

And the crazy thing is… that night in Victoria?

It was only the beginning.

From then to now, I've traveled to every major city in North America from Montreal to Miami, Vancouver to Vegas, Chicago to Cabo. I've closed deals in quiet corporate boardrooms and blown off steam in neon-lit bars that only look good after midnight. I've found myself in every dive that keeps the lights on until 2 a.m., and, when the situation dictated it, I've met clients in far less savory places where some the industry's biggest renewals have been negotiated on the back of a cocktail napkin.

Over the years, I've counseled clients through divorces, layoffs, promotions, custody battles, college decisions, marriage problems, and every category of life crisis you can think of. Sometimes they needed product answers; sometimes they needed someone who would just sit across the table, look them in the eye, and genuinely give a damn. Turns out I'd been trained for that since Leo poured Dr. Pepper in my baby bottle, at the C&W.

And somewhere along the line—maybe on flight number eight hundred, maybe on mile one million—I started staring out airplane windows, tracing highways I used to drive with my dad when life was simpler and the world felt impossibly big. Now I soar over the same roads we once crawled down in a beat-up Freightliner, and I can't help but think about how far I've come, and how none of this was supposed to happen for a kid who grew up in a bar.

That night in Victoria didn't just mark my arrival into Customer Success.

It opened the door to an entire lifetime I never saw coming, one built on earned trust, late nights, real conversations, and a million tiny moments that stitched together the life I was meant to lead.

And I'm still walking through that door today.

STOP AND REFLECT

Think back to a time when connection came before professionalism, when you dropped the formalities and just connected.

How did that change the relationship? And what would it look like to bring a little more of that authenticity into your work or your life today?

Those early days on the road taught me more than any training ever could.

I learned how to read a room, how to stay calm when everything was on fire, how to turn strangers into allies, and how to keep moving even when I was bone-tired and doubting myself.

But here's the truth I didn't understand back then:

All that experience didn't mean anything if I didn't know what I was actually trying to build.

Showing up is one thing. Showing up with intention is another.

You can't design a great career or a great life until you know what the hell you're aiming for. And most people skip that step. They hustle harder instead of digging deeper. They try to climb without knowing which wall they've leaned their ladder against.

Before you can build anything meaningful, you have to get brutally honest about who you are, what you want, and why it matters.

Alright. Let's figure out what you're really building.

CHAPTER 6
DISCOVER BEFORE YOU DESIGN

Because you can't build a plan for a life you don't yet understand.

When new CSMs join my team, they're usually eager to prove themselves.

They want to show value, host quarterly business reviews (QBRs), and roll out a success plan before they've even learned their customer's last name.

And every time, I tell them the same thing: "Don't touch the plan yet. Get on a plane. Go listen."

Because the first rule of Customer Success and of life is this: You can't prescribe before you understand.

The Steakhouse Rule

Most of the best discoveries of my career didn't happen in boardrooms or Zoom calls.

They happened across dinner tables.

It's there, over a ribeye and a pour of bourbon, that a customer finally relaxes.

The small talk fades, the posture softens, and they start talking about what's really driving them.

It's rarely just about uptime, metrics, or features.

It's about fear, ambition, pride, or redemption.

It's about wanting to prove themselves to a boss, get promoted, retire early, or just make it home for dinner without thirty emails hanging over their head.

That's when you stop talking at them and start listening to them.

That's when partnership begins.

And that same principle applies to you.

Before you build your life plan, before you architect goals and milestones, take yourself out for that same kind of dinner discovery session.

Pour a drink. Get quiet.

Ask yourself the questions you'd ask a client:

- What's really driving me right now?
- What am I afraid of?
- What do I want to feel a year from now that I don't feel today?
- What's standing in my way? And is it out there, or in here?

Don't rush the answers.

You're not building a success plan yet. You're doing discovery.

The Lunches That Changed Everything

When I was eighteen, I went to see my great uncle Dick about a job.

He was the most successful man I knew in town. He owned a cash register company, drove a nice car, and carried himself like someone who understood how the game was played.

At the time, I was making seven bucks an hour at a local computer store. I figured maybe he'd pay me eight. That extra dollar an hour felt like a raise worth showing up for.

I walked into his office one afternoon and told him I was looking for work.

He looked at me for a long moment, then said,

"I don't think you want to work here. I think you want to learn how to get rich, maybe?"

It stopped me cold. I'd never heard anyone say it like that before.

He told me that if I took him to lunch once a week, he'd teach me everything he knew about making money in America.

So I did.

With my meager paycheck, I scraped together enough to buy him lunch at a cheap Chinese restaurant down the street from his office. Over hot tea and egg rolls, he'd talk about his friends at the country club—how they bought and sold pieces of land at just the right moment or made fortunes in rental real estate.

He told me stories about how he'd built his company from nothing, one decision at a time, and how the secret wasn't working harder, it was learning how money moves, and how to become a great salesman.

Those lunches changed my entire mindset.

I walked in looking for a job.

I walked out learning how to build wealth.

It was the first time I realized that success doesn't start with opportunity; it starts with understanding what you really want before you even get started.

Do the Work, Not Just the Reflection

Reflection is the start, but it's not the whole job.

You can't just *think* your way into a new life; you've got to do the emotional heavy lifting that makes real change possible.

For me, that meant therapy.

For most of my twenties, I lived with panic attacks that would come out of nowhere—boardrooms, airplanes, even shopping malls. I thought I could outwork them. Hustle past them.

But panic doesn't care how hard you work; it's your body's way of telling you there's something underneath you haven't faced yet.

When I finally sat down with a therapist in my early thirties, I didn't want to talk about feelings.

I wanted solutions.

But what I got was understanding.

Therapy taught me how to listen to myself the same way I'd learned to listen to my clients.

It helped me see the patterns—the inherited stress, the family systems, the childhood wiring—that made me who I was.

And once I saw those patterns, I could choose which ones to keep and which ones to break.

I haven't had a serious panic attack since. And maybe more importantly, I've never stopped doing the work.

Therapy isn't a one-time tune-up. It's success planning for your soul. It's where you build emotional infrastructure that keeps your life from cracking under pressure.

The Discovery Phase Is Sacred

This phase—the listening, reflecting, healing—is not a detour.

It's part of the plan.

Because if you don't understand yourself, you'll build systems around the wrong metrics. You'll chase other people's goals. You'll end up optimizing for someone else's version of success.

Every great CSM learns to find the *why* before they chase the *what*.

The same rule applies to you.

If you want to change your life, don't start with the plan. Start with the person.

Sit with your therapist, your journal, or your reflection long enough to hear your own voice again, the version of you that's been drowned out by noise, expectations, and survival mode.

Find that person.

That's the person you're building this success plan for.

When You Understand, You Can Design

Once you know your *why*, the *how* comes naturally. You'll start to see patterns—in your habits, your relationships, your stress, your spending, your motivation.

You'll notice what gives you energy and what drains it. You'll recognize what matters and what's just noise.

That's when it's time to move from discovery to design—the same way a great CSM does after weeks of listening. That's when you can finally open the spreadsheet, map out objectives, and align your life around what truly matters.

Because now, you're not guessing. You're building from truth.

Closing Insight

The most successful people I've ever met—in business, in life—share one trait:

They know themselves.

They've sat in silence.

They've faced their shadows.

They've done the work.

And when they finally start building, they're not building from pain or panic—they're building from peace.

Because discovery isn't just how you start a Success Plan.

It's how you start becoming you.

STOP AND REFLECT

Before you start your Success Plan, ask yourself:

1. What parts of me need understanding, not fixing?

2. What have I inherited—beliefs, fears, behaviors—that I can update for the next generation?

3. Who can I talk to (a therapist, mentor, pastor or friend) to help me see myself more clearly?

4. What would my life look like if I led myself with the same empathy I give others?

Once you know what you want your life to look like, something strange happens: Your past suddenly comes into sharper focus. You start seeing the moments, the eras, the people, and the lessons that shaped you long before you ever knew you were being shaped.

Before I ever stepped into boardrooms, airports, or customer meetings, I grew up in a world that feels almost impossible now, a world without smartphones, without constant noise, without the digital leash we all *pretend* isn't choking us.

A different time. A different world. One that built a different kind of kid. If you want to understand the man I became and the values behind the systems in this book, you have to understand that era too.

Alright. Let's go back for a minute.

CHAPTER 7
THE VALLEY BEFORE THE VALLEY

Because some seeds get planted long before you know what they'll grow into.

If you want to understand the systems that eventually built my career and the life I live today, you have to understand where the spark came from. I didn't know it at the time, but everything I later built in enterprise software, every framework I use with Fortune 10 clients, every habit that drove my success... they all started here, with one small moment of curiosity in a little Northern California living room.

This isn't nostalgia. This is the origin of the mindset that changed everything.

The First Spark

The first time I ever saw a computer, I was eight years old.

It was 1983, and I was lucky enough to be growing up in Northern California—just downwind from the birthplace of Silicon Valley.

My pal Cameron asked if I wanted to play a game on his Commodore 64 after school. He said it casually, like it was a lamp. But for me, it was like looking into the future.

The colors. The sound. The possibilities.

That beige keyboard might as well have been a spaceship console.

That night I couldn't sleep. I lay in bed with my imagination on fire. I thought about things that didn't even exist yet: flying a camera through the sky, watching movies at home, talking face-to-face through a screen.

I didn't care how far out those ideas were. I had seen the future, and I wanted in.

The House That Built My Future

For weeks, I stopped at Cameron's every day after school. He got bored. I never did.

Eventually, his parents called mine to suggest that maybe, just maybe, they should get me a computer of my own, so I'd stop camping out in their living room for five hours at a time.

My parents weren't wealthy. Not even close. My dad was working long days on the road to keep food on the table, and my mom was stretching every dollar to make ends meet.

We didn't have much of value. We never took vacations. The one time we did try to go to Great America, the car broke down in the parking lot and my dad spent the entire day fixing it in one-hundred-degree heat while my mom and I rode the rides.

But somehow—and to this day I don't know how—they made it happen.

For my birthday that year, they bought me a Commodore 64 and a 1541 disk drive. It was the most beautiful thing I'd ever seen.

I hooked it up to a tiny twelve-inch TV in my bedroom, the same one I watched Saturday morning cartoons on. The screen flickered, I sat ten inches away, and none of it mattered.

This was my world now.

And with that computer came a book: *Programming Video Games in BASIC.*

That book changed everything.

Love in the Form of a Manual

When I couldn't figure something out, it was my mom who quietly showed up with answers.

After months of begging for a modem so I could connect with other users over the phone line, my parents finally relented and got me a 300 baud modem.

The first time I dialed into a Bulletin Board System (BBS), the screen stayed blank for hours. I thought I'd broken it. I tried every key. Nothing.

So, my mom took me to Waldenbooks at the mall and asked the clerk if they had a book about computers and telephones. We came home with a 350-page guide to telecommunications.

I wasn't much of a reader back then. She was.

She read the whole thing until she found the answer: "After connecting, press RETURN several times."

We tried it.

The screen exploded into ASCII art—a pirate ship, a crow's nest, a world I didn't know existed.

That one keystroke—and that one act of compassion—opened the door to everything that came next.

The Cost of Curiosity

Computers weren't cheap. Neither were floppy disks. I learned quickly that my curiosity carried a cost, and my father absorbed it without complaint.

When I needed a used 20MB hard drive from a guy in Hawaii for $800, which in today's money might as well have been $5,000, he didn't laugh. He didn't doubt me. He didn't tell me I was out of my mind.

He said: "You raise half. I'll cover the rest."

That meant more nights on the road for him. More cheap meals. More hours behind the wheel of a truck.

I mowed lawns, ran yard sales, saved every dollar. And when I hit half, Dad made good on his word.

The hard drive arrived. It didn't work.

I panicked.

I called one of my connections from the BBS community, Mike, an older Italian guy with tattoos who drove a beat-up VW bug, and he called his buddy Bob, a middle-aged Black guy on a motorcycle. Together, they fixed it: a missing jumper connection.

My mom wasn't thrilled about the characters showing up at our house, but that was the magic of the computer community back then: it brought together people who never would have crossed paths.

When the drive whirred to life, I shouted, "It works!"

And my mom smiled.

That drive became the heart of my BBS, *The Surf Board*. I became known as a competent SYSOP (system operator) before I was twelve.

The Sacrifices I Never Saw

Looking back, I see the quiet sacrifices everywhere:

The extra miles Dad drove.

The patient nights Mom sat beside me.

The way she defended my obsession when teachers complained.

The honesty in her worry when she said I was spending too much time on the computer.

And Dad's soft reply: "I don't want to do anything that hurts his chances at a career in computers. I don't want to see him driving a truck one day."

They weren't just funding a hobby. They were funding a future they hoped would be better than their own.

From 8-Bit Dreams to Real Life Lessons

I still think about that kid hunched in front of a flickering TV, typing commands into the void while the disk drive ticked and hummed.

He didn't know what he was building.

He just knew it mattered.

Looking back now, I can see exactly what those years gave me:

- The ability to solve problems when nothing works the first time.
- A deep love for learning and experimentation.
- The confidence to figure shit out on my own.
- The understanding that behind every great system is a handful of people who refuse to quit.
- A sense of belonging in a world that didn't fit into any one box.

Those were the earliest versions of everything I would later teach, refine, and use in my adult life.

The Real Lessons—Not Luck

For years I told myself I was lucky—lucky to grow up near Silicon Valley, lucky to have parents who backed me, lucky to find mentors who believed in me.

But luck isn't a plan. And luck alone doesn't build a life.

What mattered—what actually became the foundation of everything I've achieved since—were the *systems beneath the luck*:

- Curiosity
- Resourcefulness
- Persistence
- Mentorship
- Community

And the willingness to keep pressing RETURN when the screen is blank.

These aren't accidents. They're learnable. Replicable. Transferable. And they're the same systems you can build, no matter where you started.

Because success isn't built from what you're given. Success is built from what you *do with what you're given*.

Every system I use today—every framework, every decision model, every tool I teach—traces back to this beginning.

Ask Yourself:

Who sacrificed quietly to help you chase your curiosity?

When was the last time you told them how they impacted you?

Those early years in front of that Commodore 64 taught me curiosity, persistence, and how to solve problems when nothing worked the first time. But computers weren't the only place I was learning.

My real education, the one that shaped how I deal with people, money, risk, relationships, and the human side of business, happened somewhere far less predictable.

If the Commodore 64 taught me how systems work, the casino taught me how *people* work.

It was the first place I ever saw real stakes. Real adrenaline. Real winners and real losers.

A place where human behavior wasn't theoretical, it was loud, messy, emotional, and raw.

And whether I realized it or not at the time, those flashing lights and late-night conversations became the foundation for how I navigate boardrooms, billion-dollar clients, and the human psychology behind Customer Success.

Alright. Come roll the dice with me.

CHAPTER 8
WHAT I LEARNED ABOUT BUSINESS AND PEOPLE WHILE GROWING UP IN A CASINO

"Luck be a lady tonight."
—Frank Sinatra

When I turned twenty-one, I didn't run for the bars like everyone else I knew. The nightclub scene wasn't for me—too loud, too crowded, too performative.

To make things worse, honestly, I had no game, and the thought of dancing made me physically ill. Like literally, wracked with anxiety. So, there wasn't much for me to get excited about out there, when it came to typical early twenties night life.

Sure, I was very interested in meeting girls, but I really had no clue what to do or say if I met one.

Yes, dear reader, the charming, confident, road-warrior conversationalist who is known far and wide for his wining and dining skills did not exist yet, when I was twenty-one. I had yet to invent him.

Growing up with my parents' struggling relationship as my only model for love didn't exactly set me up to be Don Juan. I'd seen no hugs, no affection, and very little warmth. My only understanding of romance came from watching rom-coms, which, as I later learned, are not actually that accurate when it comes to how people fall in love.

Turns out, waiting months—or years—for the girl of your dreams to magically fall in love with you before you've actually spoken to her isn't a winning strategy. Also, the simple act of loving her from a distance will not cause her to suddenly notice you. Who knew?

So, while my friends were trying their luck on dance floors, I was about to find mine somewhere else—at the roulette wheels and craps tables of Reno, Nevada.

The Road to Reno

It started innocently enough. I had a beat-up Mustang, a college class schedule that ended Friday afternoons, and a restlessness mixed with a need to take risk that I couldn't explain. Reno was just two and a half hours from Sacramento—close enough to make it a weekend ritual, far enough to feel like another world.

My best friend Brian came along for the ride. If I was Frank Sinatra, he was my Dean Martin—always up for the adventure, always in on the bit. For being perpetually half in the bag, Brian served as a great live commentator for my life in those days, as well as a historian. I could always count on him to recount the great tales of our exploits with pizzaz when we looked back on them.

Some weekends, we'd hit snowstorms on Donner Pass, and I'd find myself out there in shorts and flip-flops, throwing tire chains on in thirty-degree weather while a highway patrolman lectured me about poor judgment. He wasn't wrong. But I wasn't about to turn around. Those were the days when the two-and-a-half-hour drive was more like five, but we powered through.

Because up ahead, beyond the snow and the dark, were the neon lights. They hit you before you even hit the city limits—pinks, blues, and flickering reds cutting through the desert air. Reno. The Biggest Little City in the World.

And to me, it was heaven.

Learning the Games

I loved everything about casinos—the hum of the machines, the sound of dice bouncing off felt, the smell of stale cigarette smoke and desperation mixed with perfume and ambition.

The people these casinos attracted were a wild spectrum of the world's best dressed and wealthiest patrons, all the way down to the dregs of society who were hanging on to the bottom rung, hoping for just that one elusive win to change their luck. More often the latter, actually.

My first game was roulette. I figured out early that betting on red or black was an even-money bet, but betting thirds of the board was where you could triple your money while still having decent odds. It felt like a math problem I could solve—an equation that could make me rich if I played it long enough.

And for a while, I did pretty damn well.

I'd drive up to Reno with $200 from my computer-store paycheck— real money to me at the time—and get treated like a high roller. Free rooms, free food, free drinks. My friend Brian, who'd sometimes only have $30 or $40 for the whole weekend, lived like a king off the comps.

I learned to bet on sports, not from other gamblers, but by befriending several of the casino dealers who always seemed to have an inside scoop on the big games. I remember becoming a basketball fan while watching Michael Jordan in the NBA finals from the sports book, reclining in a high-backed leather chair, thinking, *I am a king*, while the waitresses ran free drinks over, and picked up our Keno cards.

We discovered early that if you tip the cocktail waitress, you could keep the drinks flowing anywhere, even at the nickel video poker machines. And if you looked the part—suits, ties, confidence—the pit bosses assumed you *were* somebody. We'd dress up like we were auditioning for *Ocean's Eleven* before the new version even came out.

Those were the golden days of cheap lobster and $.99 shrimp cocktails. I couldn't understand why everyone wasn't doing this. To me, this was living—freedom, risk, laughter, and the hum of possibility.

Sometimes we'd meet other gamblers twice our age and fall in with their crew for a night on the town. Other times we met actual girls our own age, which proved that we didn't have to go to nightclubs to meet women.

The town became our playground.

Beginner's Luck

After trying a little bit of everything, the game that really hooked me was craps.

One morning I passed a dealer offering free lessons. Within minutes, I was rolling dice like I'd done it my whole life. The rhythm of it, the teamwork, the crowd energy—it felt alive. The rules didn't seem that hard, and the payouts seemed great, when you could guess the trend of the table, which I often could.

It was our last night in town, that weekend, and I was down a grand—which was, for a college kid making $500 a month, catastrophic. You could say that my appetite for taking risk had been increasing recently. On the drive home, we stopped at the last casino before the California border—Boomtown.

Boomtown isn't glamorous. It's a last-chance kind of truck-stop casino, right before you cross back into California, and if we looked like high rollers in the Reno casinos, we really looked like elite gamblers here. The waitresses looked tired; the patrons consisted of mostly truckers stopping in for the night. I believe a hotel room there was about $20 back in those days.

I pulled $200 from the ATM, feeling like my card was still smoking from the day we'd had in Reno, and joined two tired truckers at a quiet craps table. Two hours later, I walked out with $2,200.

It was one of those legendary rolls you never forget—dice on fire, cheers from strangers, pit bosses sweating. The truckers just kept handing me the dice back, knowing I was hot. When the dice would bounce off the table and land on the floor, I'd yell "Same dice!" to preserve my lucky roll. It was beginner's luck, sure, but it felt like destiny.

I drove home through the night, acting as designated driver, grinning like I'd just robbed the vault, Brian passed out in the passenger seat, having witnessed it all as the designated drunk.

When I told my parents, my mom cheered like I'd won the lottery. My dad just smiled, shook his head, and said, "Don't let them get into you for too much money."

It was the best advice I ever ignored.

Graduating to Vegas

The casino years stretched on for over a decade—through my twenties and into my thirties.

Eventually, Reno felt small. Vegas was calling, and easy to get to, once I'd moved to Colorado, thanks to $29 flights on discount airlines.

I had been in love with Las Vegas since I was a little kid, having delivered much of the marble and tile on my Dad's truck to many of the grandest casinos as they were being built in the desert. I remember the first time he told me that they were building a giant Egyptian pyramid in Las Vegas, and that I needed to join him that summer in order to see it. We ended up delivering some of the glass that went into it.

Those early Vegas trips with my friends were my chance to take a bite out of the town I helped build. They were pure chaos—six or eight of us packed into a two-queen room on Fremont Street, sleeping on floors, bathtubs, and pool loungers. We'd fall asleep recounting epic stories from our night out on the town, only to have dreams of rolling dice all night long. We'd wake up hungover, half-dressed, and laughing, ready to do it all over again.

We always dressed sharp. Suits, tuxes, our lady friends in gowns—we looked like we belonged in a movie. I remember one night at the Double Down Saloon, Brian got tossed into a mosh pit in his beige suit and came out with a giant boot print on his back. He considered it a badge of honor. His suit still carries that badge to this day.

One night I'll never forget, I quickly lost $200 on the craps table, leaving our group so I could go to the bar to grab a "free" drink by sliding $20 into a video poker machine, hoping I'd kill sometime while my luck rallied. It didn't take long; within seconds, I hit a royal flush for a $1,200 jackpot.

Another night at a little dive off the strip called the Greek Isle Casino, I got up to karaoke in my tux and sang Sinatra's "Fly Me to the Moon" to a room full of retirees and locals, before Brian took the stage and screamed Jim Morrison's "Back Door Man" until security turned off the mic. Our group yelled in protest, as they dragged him from the stage like the actual Jim Morrison. It was absurd, it was glorious, and it was pure joy.

In those days in Vegas, the food and drinks were cheap, the entertainment was always fabulous, and the nights seemed to last forever.

The Palms Era

At some point in the early 2000s, I'd graduated to the Palms—Vegas's hottest spot back when the Maloof brothers ran it, and the Playboy brand was still strong. It was common to see celebrities and Playboy bunnies there every weekend, and my casino host would give us free access to the Playboy Club and Ghost Bar anytime we wanted to go up and get a view of the city from the top. Getting to skip the line for both always made us feel like big shots, like we'd finally made it.

One of those nights, when I was once again thinking to myself, *Why doesn't everyone LOVE this town the way I do?* my friend Tim and I started a streak of wins so outrageous it borders on myth. I've been scared to even talk about it, for fear of upsetting the gambling gods.

Eleven different trips, eleven winning sessions on the baccarat table, inside the Palms. We thought it would come to an end eventually, but every time we returned to our lucky table it stayed lucky, almost like it was sitting in some sort of a gambler's vortex that could only result in good vibes.

One night, in 2019, we were winning so much that the casino sent in a professional "cooler"—a woman dressed like a human alarm bell in Mr. Magoo glasses, hauling ten shopping bags that squeaked like rubber ducks, seemingly full of bubble wrap. She looked like chaos on two legs and sat right next to us after slapping each of us with her shopping bags. She fumbled a wad of screwed up bills onto the table, which caused the dealer to stop the game and unfold them carefully so that he could issue her chips, and instantly, like any lifelong gambler would be, I was on to them, and I was pissed.

I stood up, looked at the pit boss, and said, "You think we wouldn't notice? It's 2 a.m.—where the hell has she been shopping?"

He shrugged my way, as we cashed out right there, up over ten grand. To this day, we've never gone back.

The streak lives untouched.

The Night We Discovered Elvis Costello

My buddy Brian had one of those faces—the kind that could open doors if you tilted the light just right. Dressed in a velvet tuxedo and dark sunglasses, he looked exactly like the singer Elvis Costello. I mean uncanny. None of us even knew much about Elvis

Costello's music, but that didn't matter. Vegas didn't care about accuracy; it cared about the show.

After Brian got recognized as Costello a couple of times on the Strip, an idea started to form. A bad one. The best kind.

We decided to leverage the likeness. Not for money, for status. For access. For the kind of treatment normally reserved for the real stars.

That night we rolled up to one of the hottest nightclubs on the Strip in a rented limo, split between eight of us. I walked up to the security staff, trying to look like a man burdened by celebrity responsibility, and said,

"Hey, I've got Elvis Costello out in the limo. You guys prepared for that level of action?"

Without hesitation, the guy nodded.

"Yes, sir. Please bring him in."

And just like that, velvet ropes parted, no cover charge, VIP section unlocked. They even assigned us a personal security guard and started sending over bottle service like we were royalty.

For the next few trips, we rode that wave: night after night of skipping lines, flashing smiles, and pretending to live in the alternate universe where Brian was Elvis Costello.

It all came crashing down at one club when someone overheard "Elvis" telling a wild story in a not-British accent. The jig was up. The staff realized they'd been entertaining an impersonator, and we got tossed out into the neon night, security guards laughing "Nice try!" as they did it.

It didn't matter.

For those few glorious nights, we weren't just kids playing pretend.

We were headliners.

Those nights taught me something I've never forgotten:

Sometimes the rules are meant to be broken, and if you can get a laugh while getting caught, you're playing with house money.

Love and Luck

Vegas gave me a lot of wild memories, but the most meaningful one came years later.

Trust me, the irony isn't lost on me, that my lack of game pushed me into the casino world, and that I would ultimately marry the girl of my dreams in a casino.

You're going to meet her properly in a future chapter, but let me just tease here that in 2009, I married Erin in the penthouse at Mandalay Bay, my twin daughters standing by as flower girls. The view from that suite was unreal—floor-to-ceiling glass looking straight down on the desert below, planes taking off and landing at the then-called McCarran Airport, within our view.

We'd asked the hotel to put together something simple—twenty or so of our closest friends, nothing flashy—but the moment the justice of the peace started speaking, it became something unforgettable. He said exactly what we needed to hear in that season of our lives—about love, timing, and believing in the odds when they're worth betting on.

It was a perfect Vegas moment: heartfelt, unexpected, and a little bit magical.

Luck had finally brought me to the best table of all.

When I kissed the bride, the suite sound system blasted Dean Martin's "Ain't That a Kick In The Head," and we fled the scene to start our lives.

What Growing Up in Casinos Taught Me About Business and People

All those years of neon lights and dice weren't just wild weekends—they were a masterclass in human behavior and trend analysis.

Casinos are the world's purest microcosm of business. Everything that happens on a casino floor also happens in boardrooms and sales calls—it's just louder, smokier, and served with free cocktails.

Here's what I learned:

1. People reveal who they are when they think no one's watching. At the table, you see greed, fear, joy, arrogance, humility—every human emotion, unfiltered. Business is the same. If you learn to read people, you can see the win or the loss before the dice ever hits the felt.
2. You have to stay calm when the chips are down. The best gamblers—and the best executives—don't panic. They don't chase losses. They play the long game, stay patient, and know that every streak, good or bad, eventually ends.
3. Luck is real, but discipline keeps you in the game. I've had my share of hot streaks, but what kept me out of trouble was never betting more than I could afford to lose. Or at least that's what I told myself. Same goes for business—make bold moves, but always manage your downside.
4. The loudest table usually wins. Whether in casinos or boardrooms, energy attracts energy. People want to be near momentum. If you can bring confidence, humor, and life to the room—people will bet on you.
5. The house always wins—unless you play a different game. In gambling, the odds favor the casino. In business, they favor the status quo.
   To win, you have to play on your own terms—know when to walk away, when to double down, and when to change tables entirely, or go for a lap around the building to change your luck.

Looking back now, I realize those casino nights were never about the money. They were about chasing connection, learning psychology, and understanding what makes people tick.

I didn't know it at the time, but those smoky rooms were my first MBA—my real education in reading the room, managing emotion, and playing the long game while I analyzed the trend.

And if you can do that—whether it's in Vegas, a boardroom, or a customer meeting—you'll never gamble with your future.

When I think back on all those years in casinos—the lights, the laughter, the dice bouncing off green felt—I realize it wasn't the cards or the tables that kept me coming back. It was the people. The risk. The rhythm of chance that mirrors life itself.

Vegas taught me how to bet big, lose gracefully, and celebrate when the odds fall your way. But most importantly, it taught me that some things are worth betting everything on, like love, like family, like believing in your own luck.

So, when Erin and I stood together in that penthouse at Mandalay Bay, looking down over the city that had been my playground for so long, I knew this was the best wager I'd ever made.

STOP AND REFLECT

What's the last big "bet" you made professionally? Was it guided by impulse or strategy?

Where in your life do you need to *double down*, and where do you need to *change tables*?

Are you playing by someone else's rules, e.g., your company's, your industry's, or your own?

What would change if you redefined the game?

The casino taught me more about human behavior than any text-book ever could. You see the truth fast in a place like that: People don't lose because the odds are bad, they lose because they show up with **no plan**, no discipline, no strategy, just emotion and wishful thinking.

And here's the uncomfortable part: Most adults live their lives the same damn way.

They gamble with their money. They gamble with their careers. They gamble with their relationships. They gamble with their time. All because nobody ever taught them how to think long-term or operate with intention.

That lesson stuck with me. Hard. Because if you want to win in life, you don't play blind. You play like a strategist.

That's why the same systems I use to run multi-million-dollar accounts are the systems I use to run my *life*.

If you want control, clarity, and real momentum, you start with strategy. You start with objectives. You start with a plan.

Alright. Let's get to work.

CHAPTER 9
PLAN LIFE LIKE A CSM, STARTING WITH STRATEGIC OBJECTIVES

Because grit without a plan is just slow-motion burnout.

Most people work hard.

Fewer work smart.

Almost no one builds a plan.

In business and in life, you can hustle your way into exhaustion, but not into excellence.

If you don't know what you're working toward, you're just burning fuel without direction.

That's where strategic objectives come in.

What's a Strategic Objective?

A strategic objective is a major outcome that anchors your long-term vision or North Star. If your North Star is the kind of life you wish to create for yourself, then a strategic objective is a waypoint that keeps you on the path toward ultimate success.

You don't need ten.

You need two or three that create ripple effects across your life.

Examples:

- Get into the best shape of my life and create a sustainable fitness routine in twenty-four months.
- Build $25,000 in emergency savings over twelve months.
- Repair relationship with my daughter through weekly connection.
- Get promoted to manager by Q3 through cross-functional visibility.
- Grow side income to $3,000/month by year-end.
- Find and marry my soulmate.
- Improve sleep quality so that I get eight hours a night of sleep by Q3.
- Achieve $1M in my 401(k) by year X.

Each one has leverage. Each one matters. Choose from what's most important to where your journey is headed.

The Three Filters for Choosing What Matters

Before you commit to a goal, run it through these three filters:

1. **Alignment**: Does this support your North Star?
   If your vision is about getting healthier, is eating fast food three days a week in alignment or a distraction?
   If your vision is about finding true love, can you do that without putting in the time to get to know yourself first?
   If your vision is to become wealthy, is spending every bonus on toys helping or hurting you?
2. **Leverage**: Will this create momentum in other areas?
   Becoming fit doesn't just improve health, it also boosts confidence, sharpens focus, reduces anxiety, gives you access to a larger pool of potential mates, and increases career performance.

Becoming financially stable replaces panic with power. You stop saying "someday" and start saying "I've got this." You sleep better, fight less, and finally have the breathing room to build what's next.

That's leverage.

3. **Clarity**: Can you track progress easily?

If you can't measure it, you can't manage it.

If you can't manage it, you won't achieve it.

Why Most People Get This Wrong

Most people confuse tactics with strategy.

They make to-do lists. They chase what's urgent. They feel productive, but they're not making progress.

Zoom out, and you'll see it: None of their daily actions ladder up to a meaningful outcome.

They're stuck in reaction mode.

You can't just hustle your way to a meaningful life.

You have to choose what matters, and commit to it.

My Strategic Objectives: Avoiding the Family Tradition

In my thirties, I felt it happening: that slow slide into the same pattern I'd watched my parents live through.

Working harder, not smarter.

Taking my eye off the big picture.

Confusing movement with momentum.

I was pulling long hours, making decent money, but had no clarity on why or where it was all going.

So, I hit pause.

And I wrote down three strategic objectives that would change my life forever:

1. Become physically fit and healthy.
   I'd never spent time in a gym consistently and thought meal prep meant microwaving a pouch, or throwing a can of chili on the stove.
2. Land a role in enterprise software with $100K+ earning potential.
   At the time, I was making $65K in a dead-end job and felt trapped.
3. Find and marry the love of my life before it was too late.
   I was done chasing, done guessing; I wanted partnership, purpose, and stability.

Each one required planning, discipline, and tradeoffs.

Each one changed the trajectory of my life.

That's what good objectives do.

They give you direction and purpose. They keep you from repeating generational patterns by forcing you to design your next chapter with intention.

Exercise: Define Two or Three Strategic Objectives for the Next Twelve Months

Grab a notebook.

Ask yourself:

- What are the two or three outcomes that would create the biggest transformation in my life this year?
- How do they align with my North Star?
- What's the cost of *not* focusing on them?

Write them down.

Commit to them.

Because the moment you do, you stop drifting and start designing.

We'll break these into action plans next.

What's one big objective you've been postponing, e.g., the one that would change everything if you focused on it for the next twelve months?

And what's the cost—emotionally, financially, spiritually—of continuing to wait?

Once you learn to run your life with the same discipline you bring to a $50M account, everything changes. You stop drifting. You stop reacting. You stop waking up every day wondering why nothing is moving forward. Because now you've got objectives, structure, intention—a roadmap from which to steer the damn ship.

But here's the thing most people miss:

You don't learn the value of a plan by reading a book.

You learn it by living through what happens when there isn't one.

Before I ever became a CSM, before I ever built systems or strategies or long-term thinking, I watched a man I loved run his entire life on grit alone—no safety net, no direction, no backup plan, just raw determination and a dream he tried to hold together with his bare hands.

And as much as I admire the hell out of him... that road nearly destroyed him.

If you want to understand why planning became my religion, why strategy and game theory became my oxygen, why I believe intention is the only thing that can save you from a life spinning out of control, you need to understand what drove all of that into existence.

Alright. Let me show you the miles that shaped me.

CHAPTER 10
MILES BETWEEN US

Because grit without a plan will always drive you in circles.

When my dad retired from the Air Force, in 1976, he didn't have a plan.

After twenty-two years of service across the globe—and three marriages—he came home to the States with a young British wife and a newborn son: me.

He tried a few odd jobs as motel front desk clerk, apartment manager, whatever paid something and didn't come with a boss barking orders. But nothing stuck.

Then one day, in a bar, he ran into an old friend who was driving a truck.

That conversation changed everything.

He decided he'd start his own trucking business.

A Bad Time for Big Dreams

The timing couldn't have been worse.

America was in the middle of one of its toughest recessions since the Great Depression.

Inflation was sky-high. Unemployment soared. Mortgages hit 20 percent.

We even had a national "Misery Index" to measure just how bad things had gotten.

And to top it off, there was a gas crisis. Long lines at every station. Fuel rationing. Tempers short.

But my dad had something stronger than fear: pride.

He got his sister to cosign on a ragged old International Freightliner cabover that had already logged over a million miles. It belched smoke, leaked oil, and the air conditioner was dead.

But it was his.

He became an owner-operator, and he said that title with more pride than I ever heard him use for his military rank.

That truck meant freedom.

Control.

A mission that finally belonged to him.

Riding Shotgun

In the early days, my mom and I rode along on long hauls.

I remember sitting high in the cab, looking down at the world— thinking my dad was the king of the highway.

I'd pitch him Budweiser, which he'd call *big reds*, from the ice chest up front (it was the 1970s, drinking and driving laws weren't quite a thing yet).

During the gas crisis, he'd get on the CB radio and call ahead:

"Breaker one-nine, anyone got diesel on hand?"

One station would squawk back, "Twenty gallons here."

Another would say, "I've got twenty-five."

We'd spend two hours just cobbling together enough fuel to keep moving.

The road was long.

The money was short.

But the dream was alive, at least for a while.

When the Romance Faded

For my mom, the novelty wore off fast.

The cab was rough. The rides were long. No air ride, no air conditioning, no comfort. The road was lonely, and the money wasn't as easy as they'd hoped.

When the truck broke down, she tried to make the best of it by setting up little picnics in nearby parks, pretending we were explorers on the Serengeti. Once she carved a "garage" out of a box she found in a dumpster using my Dad's pocketknife, for me to play Matchbox cars in. She had a gift for imagination. She was a dreamer at heart.

When I'd cry in the heat, she'd find a way to make it an adventure, wrapping wet towels around our heads like we were crossing the Sahara Desert.

But optimism doesn't pay repair bills.

The business bled cash. Soon, my dad was gone eleven months out of the year, sometimes home for a weekend, but rarely for a week.

I didn't see him much. But every summer, he'd let me ride along for a month.

I wasn't just there for company, I helped.

I tied the loads down. Kept the cab clean. Held flashlights when repairs had to be made on the side of the road.

I learned to recognize the sound of his engine and Jake brake from miles away.

I wanted to make him proud.

The Solo Act

When I was six, he bought a second truck to expand.

It didn't last long.

Managing maintenance on two aging rigs was hell. Managing employees was worse.

I even recruited the dad of one of my best friends to be one of our drivers, but within a couple of years, he quit, without giving notice.

Dad used to joke that the part of the business he enjoyed the least was having to deal with other truck drivers. Despite his love of independence, and the open road, he never considered himself one of them, completely.

After losing his only employee, Dad sold the second truck and went back to being a solo act.

Even then, it was brutal. Breakdowns were constant.

I remember nights when he spent every last dime to get his rig back on the road.

Once, he floated a massive repair on his green American Express card and nearly fell to his knees with gratitude when the charge went through. Technically, there was no set spending limit on green cards in those days, so he was completely at the mercy of Amex on that one.

He did all his accounting on the backs of junk mail envelopes.

We were always just about to get ahead until the next engine failed, or another crooked repair shop double-charged him for bad work that would result in the truck broken down on the side of the road, in the middle of nowhere.

The House Got Darker

Back home, things were unraveling.

Carl Lenocker

My mom wasn't built for that kind of loneliness.

She started drinking heavily, vodka mostly, and her dreams started dying, when the bipolar depression she'd fought for years started winning.

This wasn't the life she'd imagined when she left England and her eight-year-old son behind.

The optimism that carried her across the world faded.

There were stretches of silence—days when she wouldn't speak to me. I recognize now that was emotional abuse. Other days, the silence turned to rage.

I only rarely got to see the upside of living with a person with bipolar, like the time I came home from school to find she had sanded and stained all the hardwood floors in our house by herself, after moving all our furniture into the backyard single-handedly.

The house grew darker, as our nightly routine fell into some rhythm of her making sure I did my homework, then feeding me dinner, before she would drink to the point of blacking out on our living room couch.

When she passed out on the floor, I'd put myself to bed, but not before gently draping a blanket over her.

I'd hide her vodka bottle on my way to bed, way back in the cabinet, but she'd always find it the next day.

She still functioned. Still rode her bike to my elementary school most mornings to volunteer.

The teachers loved her. The kids loved her. That routine—that performance— kept her going for a while, until it didn't.

I had no understanding that none of this was normal until many years later.

Waiting for the Sound of Home

I used to ride my BMX bike to the end of our street, straining to hear the sound of Dad's truck.

Sometimes, when Mom and I weren't getting along, I'd bike over to the Sears parking lot where he parked his trailer, hoping I'd see signs of him.

If it was summertime, we'd usually be baking in our stucco oven of a house, in one-hundred-degree valley heat, because our swamp cooler was perpetually broken, and we had no air conditioning. Dad was the only one who could fix it, and god forbid my parents ever call a repairman—too expensive.

Things always got better when he came home—at least for a little while. He'd fix the swamp cooler, cheer Mom up, then he'd need to get back to the road so we could pay our bills.

When he was approaching, I could pick out the sound of his engine from miles away.

I could hear his Jake brake echoing down the highway before anyone else.

I even had a battery-powered CB radio on my handlebars.

When he got close enough, his voice would crackle through the static: "Baby Bear, this is Papa Bear, do you copy?"

That was our language.

That was love—in the only form he knew how to send it.

When the Wheels Fell Off

His trips home got fewer and farther between.

Our finances were chaos.

He sent the same amount of money on the first of every month.

It was supposed to last. It never did.

By the twentieth, Mom was broke.

Cigarettes gone. Tempers flaring. Stress spiking.

We'd walk to our local shopping mall so she could bum cigarettes from strangers.

Sometimes she'd dig through ashtrays for half-smoked ones.

I can still remember the smell. The knot in my stomach. The shame.

Other times, at month end, we'd window shop at the mall for hours, just to have something to do. I thought she was so creative, and that she came up with the idea of window shopping on her own as a fun activity, a way to play pretend. It wasn't until years later that I understood it was because we didn't have any money.

During one of those particularly difficult months, I clearly remember her making me a plate of food for dinner and sitting at the other end of the table crying, as I ate. When I asked what she was crying for and why she wasn't eating, she replied through the tears, "There's not enough."

I didn't have words for it then, but I was learning lessons most kids never get:

- What happens when you go forward without a plan
- When you chase freedom on nothing but hope
- When your business depends on one man and one machine
- When you never learn how to manage what little you've got

My dad was a good man, maybe the hardest-working man I've ever known.

But he never had a long-term strategy. Just grit.

And grit alone isn't enough when the wheels fall off, the bills pile up, and the home fires stop burning.

That's why the next step in this journey—your journey—is defining what matters most.

It's time to build your plan.

STOP
AND
REFLECT

What patterns from your family's story still echo in your own?

Which ones deserve to continue? And which ones should end with you?

Growing up with a father who was gone more than he was home taught me something sharp and unforgettable: The presence of others is a privilege, not a guarantee.

When you spend half your childhood waiting for the sound of a diesel engine coming down the road, you learn to treasure every moment of connection you get.

Maybe that's why, later in life, I started paying such close attention to the small ways people show up—the tone of their voice, the way they treat others, the look in their eyes when you speak. The little signals that tell you who someone really is.

And it's probably why the simplest gesture in the world became one of the most powerful lessons of my life: *the handshake.*

All those miles taught me about sacrifice, absence, and grit. But they also taught me to recognize character fast, because in my house, character determined whether a family stayed together or fell apart.

And the truth is, you can read more about a person in one handshake than you can in a résumé, a degree, or a LinkedIn profile.

Alright. Let's get into it.

CHAPTER 11
THE LOST ART OF THE HANDSHAKE

Because trust starts palm-to-palm, not in a PowerPoint.

By the time the road had taken me just about everywhere, I started to realize something: All the miles, airports, and steakhouse dinners had taught me more about people than any MBA ever could.

The road doesn't just show you places, it shows you character.

And the fastest way I've ever learned to read character is through a handshake.

My parents both taught me the art of the handshake from a very early age. They knew it wasn't just about grip strength, it was about presence, respect, and how you made someone feel in that single instant.

I think the first time that lesson really showed itself was in the third grade.

Our elementary school decided to host a Christmas craft fair to raise money, and my mom, running on one of her creative highs, rented a table. For a month straight, she poured herself into it. Pinecone wreaths, clothespin angels, wine-cork ornaments… our living room looked like Santa's workshop had exploded. She was determined to make something people would love, something that proved she could turn her imagination into income.

That Saturday morning, we set up early. I sat beside her, watching as people drifted by without stopping. Sales were slow. I could see the spark in her eyes starting to fade, the way it sometimes did when things didn't go her way. A single bad day could easily fire up her depression for weeks. When she stepped outside for a smoke break, I felt that familiar worry, that she'd come back deflated.

So, I did what any nervous third grader with too much energy and no plan might do: I climbed up on the table and turned into a carnival barker. "Step right up, folks! We've got everything you need for Christmas right here!"

Heads turned. People started walking over. "Is that all you want, ma'am? Maybe add an ornament for your husband?" I said with a grin, upselling like I'd been doing it for years.

I shook every hand before and after the deal, like it was a contract. Fifteen minutes later, half the inventory was gone.

When Mom came back inside, she froze. There I was, standing on the table, money in hand, smiling ear to ear, while a crowd of happy customers walked away with her crafts. "That kid is going to make a great salesman one day!" I heard one of them say to her.

That day was the first spark of something I didn't have words for yet: The realization that connection was a kind of currency, and confidence was the hand you played with. I didn't know it then, but I was learning some big-time lessons.

Beneath my mom's creative chaos and mood swings, she was always teaching me something bigger: how to carry yourself with confidence, no matter what your circumstances.

She was, after all, true to her English roots. She kept a sterling silver tea set on a high shelf in the house that nobody was ever allowed to touch. She got a great deal on it at a yard sale and shined it regularly when it tarnished. She used to say it would only get used if the Queen ever came to visit.

It was her running joke, but she was kind of serious about it too.

That tea set represented something bigger: the belief that class isn't about money; it's about how you carry yourself.

She liked to say things like, "We are not poor, we are broke; there is a difference!" I never understood why it mattered what you called it. Our situation was uncomfortable, either way.

She drilled etiquette into me from the time I could hold a fork.

"Napkin in your lap."

"Chew with your mouth closed."

And the one that stuck most of all was a quote from her mother: "We may not be rich, but we can afford soap and water."

Meaning, there's no excuse not to be clean, well-groomed, and pre-pared.

There's no excuse not to have pride in yourself, in your home, in how you show up for others.

Our house was small, but spotless. Every item had its place. If someone stopped by, whether a neighbor, a traveling salesman, or a lost friend, they were offered a cold beer or a soda, out of pure manners. If Mom was cooking, and she usually was, she'd invite them to stay for dinner.

And they often took her up on the offer. She was proud to share what little we had.

Back then, kids respected every parent in the neighborhood, not just their own.

If you got caught doing something stupid by another mom or dad, you'd get scolded just the same. That's how community worked; character was a shared responsibility.

I remember one time a schoolmate was over and she asked why his mother was always so angry with the father. He said that it was because his dad was a drunk. Everybody on that side of town knew his dad was a drunk, but it didn't matter. My Mom spanked him right there in front of me. What the kid said was true, but her tolerance for disrespecting your parents was zero.

Sometimes a family down the street, even worse off than us, would drop off their three kids so they could have a rare night alone. They'd hand my mom a single can of Chef Boyardee ravioli as if that would cover dinner for the whole crew.

Mom would just shake her head, muttering, "Oh, for God's sake," and make a giant pot of spaghetti instead. She'd feed everyone like they were her own, because that's what people of character did; they didn't keep score. They just did the right thing.

Lessons from a Thousand Handshakes and a Hundred Hotel Bars

I think about that a lot now, especially after all the hands I've shaken in my career.

At this point, I've sat across from just about every kind of person there is: CEOs in corner offices, blue-collar heroes who built the foundations those offices stand on, twenty-somethings trying to make their mark, and gray-haired veterans holding on for one last chapter.

I've shared barstools with the loud ones, quiet ones, cynics, dreamers, and every type in between. And through it all, I've learned one undeniable truth: Sitting down with people from every corner of the corporate food chain will teach you more about life than any classroom, book, or leadership seminar ever will.

People who don't get the chance to do this kind of work—to truly connect, listen, and observe—are missing out on one of life's greatest educations.

Those of us who live in this world of human connection—client dinners, hallway conversations, airport lounges, after-hours whiskey chats, occasional cigars—we breathe rarified air. We have a front-row seat to human nature in all its forms: ambition, fear, ego, compassion, and hope.

You start to realize that this job isn't just about customer success, it's about people success.

It's about reading the room, studying humanity, learning what motivates people, what breaks them, and what brings them back to life.

If you study human nature long enough, you can see it in everything—how someone orders their drink, how they treat a server, how they shake your hand. And if you can become fluent in the language of people, if you can become a great conversationalist, a modern-day Renaissance man with empathy and range, you'll never go hungry in this world.

Because the truth is, in business and in life, the people who rise the highest aren't just the smartest, they're the ones who can connect across age, gender, culture, and title.

They're the ones who can make anyone at the table feel seen, heard, and valued.

That's what separates the good from the great. And it all starts with something as simple as a handshake.

The Intangibles

There's another layer to this: the intangibles that separate average CSMs (and people) from legends.

You can easily train someone to build a dashboard, manage a renewal, or write a QBR deck.

But it's harder to teach *feel* and difficult to script charisma, presence, or timing. If it was easy, everyone would do it, so don't feel bad if this is a part of your game you need to place added focus on and really study in order to perfect.

Some have a few jokes rehearsed and ready to go, the kind that kill at just the right moment and dissolve tension in a room faster than a glass of bourbon. Some have even gone as far as to take an improv comedy class or two, in order to perfect their comic timing.

Some do their homework before ever shaking hands, e.g., they've researched the client, found mutual acquaintances, maybe a shared alma mater or club membership. They come in prequalified for connection.

Others are accomplished listeners. They come armed with power questions that open people up, make them feel understood, and turn a casual chat into a meaningful conversation. Those I have met who are super skilled at listening have gone so far as to take acting classes, so they can ensure the look on their face matches the empathy in their heart, as they are silently listening.

Then there are the big personalities. The ones who can fill a room and keep it lit for hours, storytelling, laughing, making everyone feel like they're part of something special.

Some are the meticulous planners. They track every action item, every milestone, and can pull progress metrics from thin air like magicians. Many of these are your project management professionals or folks who have studied program management extensively throughout their careers.

Some can decode a wine list and pick the perfect bottle, not the most expensive, but the one with a story. The kind that connects your client to a memory, a vineyard, a moment. I once worked for a VP who went so far as to get his sommelier certification, simply so he could have better conversations with our clients who also love wine.

Others know how to order appetizers as an art form, transforming an ordinary dinner into a night people still talk about years later. They invite the waitress over, and expertly ask for recommendations while flushing out what the restaurant is truly known for, and what should be stayed away from on the menu.

And then there are the rare ones, the ones who connect so deeply that business becomes personal. I call these the *natural empaths*. Not because empathy is something that can't be learned if you apply yourself to this dark art, but some come across so natural that you assume it was a gift they were simply born with. Spoiler alert: Most were not born with it and actually have studied hard to master this part of their craft.

They're the ones who get invited to weddings, graduation parties, even funerals.

The ones clients call for advice when their marriage is falling apart or when they're scared about a career move.

That level of connection can't be faked, and in fact is very real, because it's earned through character, consistency, and showing up as a human being first, a professional second.

Those are the so-called intangibles. That's what the greats have in common, whether they're CSMs, CEOs, or the guy behind the bar remembering your name and your drink.

Character Can't Be Faked

The truth is, you can tell everything you need to know about someone by how they greet you.

Do they look you in the eye?

Do they smile with their eyes, not just their mouth?

Do they listen before they speak?

Or are they scanning the room for someone more important?

Because a handshake isn't just about manners, it's a mirror of your character.

And character is built long before you ever step into a boardroom.

It's forged in homes where kids are taught to clean up after themselves, to say thank you, to shake a hand firmly and mean it.

Character is what you do when nobody's watching. It's showing up on time when the flight's delayed, paying for dinner when nobody expects it, and taking responsibility when things go wrong.

It's the sum of a thousand small habits, each one shaping the person who shows up for that handshake years later.

Or maybe it's formed from getting spanked by the mom down the street, for disrespecting your parents.

Over the years, I've come to realize that relationships—in business and in life—are built the same way a house is: one brick, one handshake at a time. And if you build those foundations strong enough, they can outlast careers, companies, even decades.

Because a good handshake doesn't just introduce you. It represents you.

It's this simple: Step in with intention, look them in the eye, give one firm squeeze—not a death grip, not a limp fish—and hold it just long enough to say, without words, "I'm here, I'm solid, and you can count on me."

STOP AND REFLECT

When you walk into a meeting or shake a hand, what message are you sending before you ever speak?

Would people describe your presence as confident, distracted, or genuine?

Think of one relationship in your work life that needs rebuilding.

What small, genuine gesture could you make this week to restart that trust?

Learning how to read people—how they shake your hand, how they carry themselves, how they treat others—is one thing. Living through the consequences of *not* being able to read your own life is another.

Because no matter how good you are with people... no matter how sharp your instincts are... no matter how strong your character is... *none of it protects you from the chaos you create when you don't have direction.*

A good handshake can open doors, build trust, and change your career. But character alone won't save you if your life has no structure, no strategy, and no plan.

And the truth is, my climb didn't start with confidence or connection. It started in the wreckage—in debt, bad decisions, busted rentals, broken relationships, and one U-Haul full of furniture I should've burned in the driveway.

If the handshake chapter was about the *intangibles* that make people powerful... this next chapter is about the *mess* that forced me to learn discipline, focus, and financial resolve the hard way.

Alright. Let's hitch up the U-Haul...

CHAPTER 12
REAL ESTATE, RELATIONSHIPS, AND RESOLVE

Because the climb doesn't start with luck, it starts with chaos.

People love to romanticize "the rise." The hustle. The grind. The fist bumps at closing time.

But the truth?

My climb to my first million in net worth was a beautiful disaster.

Ya, it's true what they say: The first million is the hardest. There is no doubt about that.

But it didn't start with spreadsheets or startup equity. It started with a U-Haul full of crap furniture I should've set on fire.

Here's how I took the long road from broke to breathing room.

The Reset

My first real job out of college was with Hewlett-Packard in Colorado Springs. I definitely took the long road getting there.

To say I wasn't a great student in college would be a bit of an understatement. Luckily for me, I lived at home with my parents in

Sacramento during the experience, or I probably would have never graduated.

Due to my propensity for staying up until the early hours, exploring every corner of the early internet, I had a rough time making it to class. Mom would dutifully drag me out of bed in the morning, I'd shower, get in my car and drive to campus at Sacramento State, and there I'd usually find a shady spot in the parking garage to park, then would proceed to sleep for another two to three hours, usually until the heat woke me up.

Occasionally my mind would wander, and I'd skip driving to campus all together, finding myself standing in the self-improvement section of the nearby Barnes & Noble, flipping through the latest bestsellers. Once, I felt a swat on my rear end and turned to find my mother standing in the aisle fuming behind me. After that, I started going to class more regularly.

I can honestly say that without her, I would probably never have graduated at all.

Fast-forward to when I got the job offer. Adult life was getting off to a rough start. Even though I was living at home, and had few bills, I was trying to dig out of a mountain of credit card debt—the kind of debt that comes from a string of bad choices and zero planning.

Bad choices like taking out cash advances to trade dot-com stocks, and then trying to win my losses back on the craps tables in Reno on the weekends.

I'd been working as a contractor at HP Roseville, in Northern California, for a meager hourly wage, when the permanent job offer came in.

I was twenty-three years old and hadn't been for a run on the truck in probably five years, but Dad asked me to join him on one last trip on the truck to discuss the opportunity. As we rode up to Portland and back, he laid out strong support and said this seemed like too good of a deal to pass up. He had been stationed in Colorado

Springs during his time in the Air Force, and he convinced me that it was a great town, and HP was a good company.

The next morning, I signed on.

HP gave me a signing bonus: $23,000.

I used nearly all of it to get out of that hole of debt. It was the first financial breath I'd taken in years.

This was back when HP still cared about culture, when the "HP Way" meant something. You could feel Bill Hewlett's and Dave Packard's fingerprints on the place. It was routine to run into people who had forty years of seniority there. That said a lot.

I loaded everything I owned into that U-Haul—flea market furniture, hand-me-down pots and pans, and emotional baggage—and drove east to Colorado, with Dad, who helped me get moved.

It was a reset.

A blank slate.

I was broke, but I wasn't in debt.

And at twenty-three, that felt like wealth.

The First House

Within a year, I bought my first home, a half-duplex on the wrong side of town for $92,000.

My apartment rent was about to go up, and I hated the idea of paying more to make someone else rich. This would not stand.

I learned that as a first-time buyer, I only needed a 2 percent down payment. My mortgage would cost the same as rent, $700 a month.

So, I did it.

For $1,840 down, I controlled a $92,000 asset.

When I talked the seller into paying all my closing costs, I got a rush I'd never felt before.

That deal changed everything.

Not because it was glamorous; it wasn't.

But because it gave me leverage.

I wasn't *just* a tenant anymore.

I was an *owner*.

An *investor*.

That subtle shift in identity opened a door I didn't even know I'd been looking for.

The Real Estate Hustle

Between twenty-three and thirty-three, I went on a tear.

Before the housing market went crazy, getting a mortgage was laughably easy. If you could sign your name, you could buy a house.

So I did. Again and again.

At my peak, I owned about ten properties.

I thought I was playing Monopoly.

I thought I was a genius.

Then the 2008 crash came and reminded me I wasn't, and those types of easy loans dried up quickly.

Lessons from the Trenches

Those houses were the best education I ever got.

I learned how to manage risk. How to negotiate. How to fix a garbage disposal and unclog a sewer line at 1 a.m. How to install drywall, and why you should just pay someone to do that instead.

And how fast a tenant and their pets can destroy what took you years to build.

One woman kept two Rottweilers locked in a room, chewing through drywall and carpet.

Another stopped paying for trash pickup and dug a trench in the backyard to bury months of garbage. A third threw drug-fueled parties, where the police would come and break down both doors and leave me with a property that I couldn't even lock up.

I found out most of it after they moved out, along with roaches, broken windows, blood, and the smell of regret.

I didn't know whether to laugh, cry, or sell out and move to the mountains.

But I didn't quit.

I cleaned it up.

I moved on.

I learned.

That's what builders do.

Years later, real estate makes up around half of our net worth. Sticking with it through the ups and down was difficult, but once we reached that escape velocity where rents and appreciation started to increase, and the properties started to pay themselves off more rapidly over time, our net worth surged.

All in all, real estate has been one of the best hedges we could have asked for, because in many years when the stock market has been down, our real estate investments have still been up. Some years both go up. Some years, both go up a lot!

No matter what happens, we'll always have that cash flow to help propel us into retirement when we're ready, and the calm that comes with knowing that is like no other I've experienced.

Don't get me started on the tax benefits real estate brings. In *Rich Dad Poor Dad*, Robert Kiyosaki did a much better job of explaining it than I ever will be able to, but if you want to dive deeper, I can't recommend his book highly enough. It changed my life.

A Personal Crash

While my business life was grinding forward, in those days, my personal life was in free fall.

I didn't grow up with a great model for relationships. Having a long-haul trucker for a dad was basically like being raised by a single mom.

So, I had to figure out love on my own; and in my twenties, I got it wrong. A lot.

Low self-esteem and lack of direction led to more bad-date stories than anyone needs to hear.

There was the "massage therapist" who didn't own a massage table. Spoiler: She wasn't a therapist. At least not the type that practices with any sort of state issued license.

The woman from the internet who flew in to see me every month, until I realized she was probably married. The strange phone calls she received regularly from an angry man, and how protective she was over her cell phone were dead giveaways.

And then the one I had kids with—the fun, dramatic, chaotic one. The life of the party.

She was a broken dreamer in the same ways my mother had been, and I wasn't in a place to see that just yet.

When she was up, she could light a room on fire.

When she was low, she could burn the house down.

I thought I could fix her, take care of her like I did my mom.

You can guess how that turned out.

In 2003, we accidentally had twin girls. I was twenty-seven.

My world cracked open.

Most people cry tears of joy when their kids are born.

I cried out of fear. It felt like the walls were closing in on me.

I knew how hard this road would be. I could already see the future financial damage, the fights, the heartbreak.

I wasn't ready to be a dad, but ready or not, it was happening.

A New Mission

The relationship didn't last. She moved out when the twins were six months old. But the consequences stayed.

I suddenly had shared custody, two daughters, and $1,000 a month in child support. That was nearly everything left after my mortgage and bills. And for the first time in my life, it wasn't about me anymore.

I was scared. I was ashamed. But I didn't disappear. I worked. I pointed every ounce of ambition toward providing. I stopped chasing money and started building a future for them, for me.

Part of that future meant founding an eBay business in my garage, to make ends meet. If selling cheap Chinese trinkets on the internet was what I had to do to feed my kids and have a little left over each month to invest, then that was the plan.

I decided I wasn't just raising twin girls. I was building a dynasty. I needed to build a legacy I could leave them one day. It had to start with me.

I'd break the family cycle. Be a better father than my dad ever got the chance to be. I'd see both girls through college. I'd build new family traditions from scratch.

And one day, I'd find a partner who would make our family even stronger.

Why the First $100K Really Is the Hardest

Here's the truth no one tells you: The first $100K isn't just hard financially, it is also hard personally.

It's built on sacrifice, sleepless nights, busted rentals, and overdue bills.

It's forged in bad choices and quiet moments of resolve.

You don't earn it just in dollars, you earn it in identity.

Because just like Vegas, you can't play the game until you've got some chips on the table.

That first $100K is your stake and your ticket through the casino doors.

And once you cross that line, you'll never see money or life the same way again.

What's one hardship or financial mess from your past that taught you more than any class or book ever could?

And how can you honor those lessons by using them to build the next chapter of your life, but intentionally this time?

Climbing out of the wreckage of my twenties—the busted rentals, the bad relationships, the debt, the late-night repairs, the surprise twin daughters, the U-Haul full of broken furniture—taught me one lesson I couldn't ignore: *You can hustle your way into progress, but you can't hustle your way into a stable life.*

I had grit. I had work ethic. I had desperation breathing down my neck. But none of that was enough.

Because grit without structure is chaos. And chaos doesn't compound, it consumes.

It wasn't until I learned how to take the big picture, the vision, the goals, the dreams, and break it down into *weekly execution* that everything finally started clicking into place.

Not overnight. Not magically. But consistently, one task, one deadline, one Friday at a time.

If the last chapter showed you the fire, this next one shows you the blueprint.

Alright. Let's turn your vision into something you can truly *build*.

CHAPTER 13
BREAK IT DOWN: FROM VISION TO WEEKLY EXECUTION

Because motivation fades, but systems don't.

There's a reason most people never hit their goals. It's not because they're lazy, unmotivated, or cursed. It's because they never operationalize their vision.

They dream about the mountaintop, but they never build the steps to climb it.

In the software world, I've seen billion-dollar visions collapse because nobody owned the next action item. No due date. No clarity. Just a vague hope that if the team stayed outrageously positive and delusional, something great would eventually happen.

Sound familiar?

Your life works the same way.

Big visions are easy to post on a wall.

Execution, week after week, is where the real work happens.

So, let's break it down. Literally.

1. Start with the Vision

Everything begins with a North Star: Those big, overarching objectives we talked about earlier.

A clear, specific statement of what you actually want.

Forget fluffy stuff like "live my best life."

What does that mean in the real world?

Is it:

- Making enough money to walk away from work you don't love?
- Having the energy to chase your kids around without gasping for breath?
- Finally starting that business idea you've been talking about for years?
- Maybe a combination of all of the above?

Whatever it is, say it out loud. Write it down like it's a mission statement for your own company (because it is).

Example:

"In the next twelve months, I will build a life of strength, independence, and connection, becoming financially free, physically fit, and deeply aligned with my partner."

That's your Vision. It's your ARR (ambition, resilience, and relationships), the same framework I use in customer success.

Ambition defines where you're going. Resilience defines how you'll get up when you fall. Relationships define who's coming with you.

2. Define the Objectives

A Vision without measurable Objectives is just a wish list. Objectives are your major outcomes for the quarter or year, the *what* of your plan. Keep it tight: three to five Objectives max.

Example:

- Health: Run a 10K without stopping.
- Wealth: Save $10,000 by December.
- Relationships: Take a weeklong trip with my partner—phones off.

Each one needs a clear success metric. You wouldn't accept a customer saying "We want to improve cyber security" without defining what that means. Apply the same logic here.

---

3. Break Objectives into Initiatives

Initiatives are the bridges between the dream and the doing.

They're not tiny tasks yet; they're the big levers that drive progress.

Let's take the "Save $10,000" objective.

Initiatives could be:

1. Cut $500 a month in expenses.
2. Increase income by $500 a month.
3. Invest $5,000 for compound growth.

Now you're not just *hoping* to save money, you've got three distinct engines pulling that train.

---

4. Turn Initiatives into Tasks

Here's where the magic happens. Tasks are what you can physically do this week.

If you can't schedule it on your calendar, it's not a task, it's still an idea.

I use what I call the Success Plan Task Table. It looks like this:

Objective	Initiative	Task	Owner	Date	Status
Save $10K	Cut expenses	Cancel unused subscriptions	Me	Jan 14	✅
Save $10K	Increase income	Apply for freelance project	Me	Jan 21	🔄
Improve health	Train for 10K	Run 3 miles, 3x this week	Me	Jan 20	✅
Strengthen marriage	Plan trip	Research 3 locations	Partner	Feb 1	⧗

You'll notice three key things:

1. Every line has an owner.
2. Every line has a date.
3. Every line has a status.

If a task doesn't have those three things, it doesn't exist.

---

5. Assign Ownership

One of my favorite sayings: "If it doesn't have an owner, it doesn't exist."

In Customer Success, every milestone has a DRI—a Directly Responsible Individual.

Your life deserves the same level of accountability.

You might own your overall goal, but that doesn't mean you have to do everything.

Delegate tasks to your spouse, a friend, a coach, or even an app.

For example:

- You own the fitness goal.
- Your trainer owns the workout plan.
- Your spouse owns meal prep.

Everyone plays a role, but accountability always rolls up to you.

You're the CEO of your own life. Act like it. Own everything, at a high level.

---

6. Put Dates on Everything

Time turns ideas into outcomes.

A task with no due date is just a wish.

I call this the "Next Friday Rule."

If it's not due by next Friday, it's not real.

This keeps momentum high and procrastination low.

Weekly deadlines force movement—even small steps compound faster than perfect plans delayed.

Want to write a book? Cool. Don't set "Finish manuscript by December."

Instead:

- Outline Chapter 1 by next Friday.
- Write 500 words by next Friday.
- Edit intro by next Friday.

Repeat.

The mountain disappears one foothold at a time.

---

7. Run Weekly Reviews

Here's where you close the loop—your Personal Standup Meeting.

Every Sunday (or whatever day you like), spend fifteen minutes asking yourself three questions:

1. What's done?
   Celebrate wins, no matter how small.

(Progress releases dopamine. Let yourself feel it.)
2. What's blocked?
   Identify friction points before they become excuses.
   (Didn't run because of rain? Move to treadmill plan.)
3. What's next?
   Choose three to five tasks to move forward this week.
   No more, no less.

Consistency beats intensity. Always.

If you want to go deeper, pair this with a monthly QBR, your own Quarterly Business Review for life. Review your objectives, update your metrics, and reset your focus.

---

8. Toolkits and Systems

Systems beat willpower. Every time. Here are a few I use personally (and in my coaching work):

▦ Weekly Dashboard - A one-page Google Sheet tracking your Objectives, Initiatives, and Tasks.

▦ Success Journal - Jot down one win and one lesson per day. It keeps the feedback loop alive.

☺ Accountability Partner - Find someone who will call you out when you drift.

⚙ Automation Tools - Use task apps, calendar reminders, or templates to stay consistent.

Pro tip: Keep everything visible. What's out of sight is out of mind, and what's out of mind never gets done.

---

9. The Bigger Picture

Here's the truth:

Most people overestimate what they can do in a week and underestimate what they can do in a year. This chapter isn't about building another to-do list. It's about engineering your momentum.

When you break your vision into weekly execution, you're creating a rhythm, a drumbeat that keeps your goals alive. Every big transformation I've seen, whether in business, health, or relationships, comes down to this: Somebody somewhere decided to stop thinking and start scheduling.

So, break it down. Make it visible. Give it a date. And watch how fast your life starts compounding.

Because the truth is simple: "Success doesn't happen at once. It happens every time you decide to do the next right thing and actually put it on the calendar."

Chapter Summary: The Execution Ladder

Level	Focus	Time Horizon	Tool
Vision	The "Why"	1–10 years	Success Plan Canvas
Objectives	The "What"	Quarterly	Metrics Tracker
Initiatives	The "How"	Monthly	Initiative Tracker
Tasks	The "Now"	Weekly/Daily	Task Table
Review	The "Reflect"	Weekly & Monthly	Standup + QBR

Bottom Line

The difference between a dreamer and a doer isn't talent, it's follow-through.

You can have the perfect plan, the best tools, and the strongest motivation...

But if you don't break it down, from vision to weekly execution, you'll never see results.

So, grab your notebook, open your calendar, and start mapping your next seven days.

One week at a time, one Friday deadline after another, and you'll realize the power that's been sitting inside you all along.

Look at your biggest goal right now.

Does every step have an *owner*, a *due date*, and a *status*, or are you still hoping someone (maybe Future You) will handle it?

Write down your top objective for this quarter.

Now list three initiatives and one task you could start *this week* to move it forward.

(If you can't schedule it, it's not real.)

If you don't bring that same precision into your relationships, you'll build a life that looks great on paper and empty everywhere else.

You can run task tables, dashboards, QBRs, and weekly standups until your Google Sheet catches fire, but if your personal life is chaos, the whole system collapses.

I learned that the hard way.

I had the hustle. I had the ambition. I even had the blueprint. But when it came to love?

I was winging it, guessing, hoping, choosing partners by accident instead of intention. And nothing will derail your success faster than the wrong person beside you… or the right person finding you unprepared.

The truth is simple: Your partner is the most important "strategic hire" you'll ever make.

More important than your boss, your mentors, or your investors. The wrong hire will bankrupt your emotional bandwidth. The right one will multiply your entire life.

So, after learning how to design my goals, I had to learn how to design something far harder: Love.

Not the alcohol-fueled, swipe-right kind. Not the hope-it-works-out-this-time kind. The intentional kind. The this-is-my-vision-and-this-is-the-life-I'm-building kind.

And that's where the next chapter begins, with the moment I realized the most powerful success plan in the world means nothing…

…if you don't also success-plan your heart.

CHAPTER 14
LOVE BY DESIGN

*Because the most important decision you'll ever make is
who you build with.*

People think love just happens. That it's fate. Timing. Chemistry.

But here's what I've learned: The partner you attract is often a reflection of who you are.

And in my case, I had to become the man who would attract the kind of woman I wanted to spend my life with.

Designing the Woman of My Dreams

At one point after a string of broken relationships I got brutally honest with myself.

I stopped blaming others. I stopped coasting. And I started planning the same way I would plan a career move or a real estate investment. Because dating without intention had left me with enough bad-date stories to fill a Netflix special.

You name it, I'd seen it.

- I once dated a woman who faked a pill overdose, on my couch, as a diversion when I asked if she was seeing other guys.

- Another took infidelity so seriously she built an entire double life out of her parents' basement. Honestly, the dedication was impressive—terrifying, but impressive.
- A few bragged about being homeowners until I discovered they were renters. One even asked me to pay her rent, after being caught in the lie.
- A couple had criminal records they conveniently left off the get-to-know-you portion of our relationship.
- And then there were the ones who took one look at my life—a tired, lonely single dad just trying to keep the wheels on, and said, "Yeah… no thanks." Hard to blame them. I probably would've walked too.

When you don't date with a goal in mind, it's no surprise when you waste years on people who don't deserve your time. It's sad, but true.

So, I got intentional.

I sat down and wrote out everything I wanted in a life partner:

- Smart
- Driven
- Healthy
- Beautiful
- Financially stable
- College-educated
- Homeowner
- Career-oriented
- Traveler
- Emotionally intelligent
- Someone who wanted to build with me
- Someone who would love and support my daughters

Then I asked the hard question: "Am I the kind of man a woman like that would be excited to meet?"

The answer at the time? Not quite yet.

So I went to work on *me.*

I stripped everything down to the studs and took a hard look at the truth: My habits were sloppy, my confidence was inconsistent, my money wasn't where it needed to be, and my mindset was running on fumes.

If I wanted a world-class partner, I needed to become a world-class man. Not someday, *now*.

So, I rebuilt the whole damn operating system.

I lived in the gym like it was a second job. I inhaled every self-help book I could get my hands on. Business news replaced sitcom reruns. Podcasts replaced mindless noise. *The Wall Street Journal* hit the table every morning like a contract I had to sign with myself.

And yeah, I even read the pickup-artist stuff. Not to run game, not to manipulate anyone, but to understand how to actually talk to women with confidence instead of stumbling through every conversation like a rookie.

Then I went out into the dating world and practiced. Reps. Just like the gym. Learning how to hold a conversation, how to listen, how to show up with presence instead of desperation so that when the real opportunity showed up, I wouldn't choke.

Brick by brick, I rebuilt my habits. My finances. My confidence. My mindset.

I stopped chasing and started becoming the kind of man a phenomenal woman would actually notice.

And not long after that, I met Erin.

Meeting Erin

Erin had everything on that list and more.

She was confident, grounded, and drop-dead gorgeous, with her own rhythm. She worked hard, so hard she almost didn't have time to take my call, and she seemed to bend the universe to her will.

She was fit, fabulous, and owned her own home. Kind. Sharp. Independent. Open.

She didn't need saving. She didn't want chaos. She wanted partnership.

And for the first time in my life, I was ready for that kind of woman. If I wanted someone like Erin, I needed to show up with value or forget about it.

From our first date, I knew she was the one. When she suggested we see each other the following weekend, I didn't hesitate: "I'm not going to be able to wait that long to see you again. How about tomorrow?"

Before long, we were inseparable. We've been that way ever since, seventeen years and counting.

The Foundation of Everything

From day one, she didn't just love me, she believed in me.

I'd never experienced unconditional support like that before, and I was finally ready to receive it.

She became an incredible stepmother to my daughters, not by trying to replace anyone, but by showing up, consistently, with love and patience. She expanded our family. She didn't rewrite it.

Erin inspired me to go back and finish my MBA. To find a better job. To become the man she already saw in me.

She encouraged me, gently but persistently, to stop apologizing for wanting more. To take myself seriously again. And then came the test.

The Honeymoon Hangover

We'd just returned from our honeymoon. A honeymoon and a wedding that I had to flip a house in order to afford. The chips seemed to be falling my way for the first time in a long time.

I was feeling more confident than ever, because I had taken a gamble and won, on a very rundown house in a decent neighborhood, that turned into a quick ninety-day $30K profit. We covered all our wedding costs, and the honeymoon, and still had cash left over.

Then we got the bad news.

Literally the Monday after we got back, I was sitting at my desk, easing into my inbox when a message popped up:

"Carl, you got a sec?" from my boss.

Before I could respond, the phone rang.

"Hey man. I'm really sorry. We gotta let you go."

"What?"

"It's not personal. It's just business. Your job's being moved to India."

"You realize I just got back from my wedding and honeymoon, right?"

"Yeah, I know. I'm sorry."

Welcome to married life. I wish I could say that was the worst of it, but it was just the beginning.

The Year Everything Went Wrong

Within weeks, I was served papers to appear in family court. My ex had decided that my new marriage meant it was time to revisit our custody agreement.

What had once been an amicable coparenting arrangement, based on a handshake, suddenly turned into a full-blown legal battle. Any extra cash we had immediately was spent on lawyers.

On top of that, the stress wrecked my health. I lost forty pounds in six months. My stomach hurt constantly. I was convinced I was dying.

It was, without question, the hardest year of my life.

But Erin?

She didn't flinch.

She didn't panic.

She said, "We'll figure it out. We've got this."

And she meant it.

The Rebuild

So, I went to work. Harder than ever.

I hired an attorney and fought through a six-month court battle to secure my parental rights. We found the best doctors. Erin was at every appointment, every test, every moment.

The verdict? Stress. Pure and simple. So, I used it and decided to make some changes in my life.

I gave up soda cold turkey, which was no small feat for a kid who grew up in Silicon Valley pounding Jolt Cola at midnight and Coke for breakfast.

I cleaned up my diet. Doubled down on fitness.

Then I landed a job with a software reseller, commuting sixty miles each way. I started collecting certifications like baseball cards. It was a long shot, but I knew this could be my steppingstone to where I wanted to end up.

Within a year, I broke into the enterprise software business doubling my income overnight. I thought they were kidding when the offer letter said $110K.

When I asked my doctor if he thought I was healthy enough to start, he smiled and said, "You're ready."

And just like that, the pain in my stomach disappeared.

That job changed our lives. That woman changed mine.

You Can't Delegate Your Relationship Strategy

People make business plans. Meal plans. Retirement plans.

But when it comes to their most important relationship, they wing it.

Don't.

Choose your partner the way you'd choose a cofounder, with vision, clarity, and intention. Marriage isn't the reward. It's the starting line.

And everything you build after depends on how solid your foundation is.

I don't just love Erin, I trust her with everything I am.

If I ever achieve anything extraordinary, it'll be because of the foundation she helped me pour, one choice, one conversation, one moment of belief at a time.

STOP AND REFLECT

What kind of person are you becoming? And who are you becoming that person for?

If you designed love with the same clarity and purpose as your career, what would that look like?

If your relationship were a startup, would you invest in it?

Does your partnership have shared vision, clear roles, and mutual accountability? Or are you running on chemistry alone?

Becoming the man Erin would eventually choose wasn't luck. It wasn't fate. It was work—quiet, private, and sometimes painful work. The kind you do alone in the gym, in the mirror, in the pages of a book, telling yourself the truth whether you like it or not.

And somewhere in all that effort, I started to see a bigger pattern. I wasn't just trying to be a better partner someday. I was trying to build a better life—piece by piece, quarter by quarter, long before I ever heard her name.

The discipline, the routines, the mindset… it wasn't new. It was already in motion, already shaping who I was becoming. Erin was just the proof that the work mattered.

So, this next chapter isn't a shift; it's a reveal—how the same heart, grit, and intentionality I put into love is the same blueprint I use to run the rest of my life.

CHAPTER 15
RUN YOUR LIFE LIKE A BUSINESS

Because long-term goals are just dreams without deadlines.

My dad ran a trucking business the old-school way. His office was the dashboard of an aging Freightliner. His filing system? The backs of junk mail envelopes. His project management tool? A weathered spiral-bound logbook—filled with enough edits, white-outs, and creative date stamps to make the highway patrol weep.

He didn't just track miles and routes. He gamed the system.

Truckers were supposed to drive ten hours a day, max. But that kind of rule didn't put food on the table. So, my dad would carefully rewrite his logs in the sleeper cab while pretending to search for them during roadside stops. I remember vividly: the flashing lights, the knock on the driver's door, the officer asking for records. Dad would stall, rummaging through paperwork, while quietly rewriting his shift hours with just enough plausible deniability to avoid a ticket.

He was a master of improvisation. He could stretch time, bend rules, and outrun the system, and did so for his entire trucking career.

As brilliant as he was at surviving the moment, he never built a plan to win the long game.

From Envelopes to Execution

That image stuck with me for years: my dad, covered in diesel smoke, hunched over a paper logbook, rewriting reality to fit a broken system.

I didn't judge him. He did what he had to do. He hustled harder than any man I've ever known. But I also knew I wanted to do it differently.

I didn't want to *survive* the month. I wanted to *own* the year. I didn't want to hustle blindly; I wanted to move strategically. And I sure as hell didn't want to rewrite my numbers after the fact to make things look good.

That's when I stole an idea from business and applied it to life: the Quarterly Business Review.

The QBR Mindset: You Are the Business

In enterprise software, the QBR is sacred. It's where we pause the daily grind, pull back the curtain, and ask the hard questions:

- What outcomes did we promise?
- What value did we deliver?
- Where are we ahead?
- Where are we bleeding out?

No fluff. No excuses. Just a clear-eyed look at the truth. And that's exactly what most people don't do with their lives.

They set goals in January, grind through chaos, and hope December feels different.

But without structured reflection, every year becomes a rerun of the last.

Running your life on quarters changes that. Every ninety days, you step out of the driver's seat, climb onto the hood, and look at the road behind you. Then you decide—*what's next?*

Your Life QBR: The Framework

You don't need a boardroom. You need a quiet space, a notebook, and brutal honesty.

Here's the playbook:

1. Schedule It Like It Matters

Block one day every ninety days—no distractions, no errands, no emails. Call it your "Personal Offsite."

If you can, get out of your normal environment. A coffee shop. A cabin. A hotel lobby with a good wine list.

This isn't a to-do list review. It's a strategic reset.

2. Start with the Data

Pull up the facts from the past quarter. No feelings yet. Just the numbers.

- What did you actually accomplish?
- How did you spend your time?
- What did you earn, save, or invest?
- How often did you work out, call family, unplug?

In business, we say: "You can't manage what you don't measure."

Your life deserves the same precision.

3. Run the QBR Questions

I break my review into four quadrants—the same way I'd structure a client QBR deck:

1. Objectives & Outcomes:
   What commitments did I make this quarter?
   Which ones did I hit? Which did I miss?
2. Wins & Impact:
   What results am I proud of?
   Who benefited from my work or effort—family, clients, team, self?

3. Risks & Gaps:
   Where did I drift?
   What blind spots or bad habits showed up again?
   What resources did I need but didn't have?
4. Roadmap Ahead:
   What will I start, stop, and continue next quarter?

Write your answers honestly, like you're preparing a report for your own Board of Directors.

Because you are.

4. Score Yourself Like an Executive

Use a simple red-yellow-green system:

Category	Score	Notes
Health	Yellow	Improved workouts but sleep's off.
Finances	Green	Met savings goal early.
Relationships	Red	Date nights fell off the radar.
Career	Yellow	Strong performance, weak boundaries.

Visual feedback beats vague feelings.

Seeing too much red? That's not failure—it's clarity.

5. Write the Executive Summary

Every QBR ends with a single slide that answers: "So what?"

Write one paragraph summarizing your quarter. Be honest, but forward-looking.

Example:

"Q2 started strong but fizzled in focus. Financially on track, but energy and connection suffered. Next quarter's focus: health routines, marriage time, and better work boundaries."

Print it. Read it every Sunday. It becomes your compass.

6. Schedule Mid-Quarter Checkpoints

Executives don't disappear for three months between reviews, and neither should you.

Midway through each quarter—around the six-week mark—schedule a thirty-minute self-check.

Ask the following:

- Am I tracking to my QBR goals?
- Have priorities shifted?
- What needs reforecasting?

Think of it like a pipeline review for your life.

7. Run the QBR With Your Partner (Optional but Powerful)

If you're in a relationship, this is a game-changer and can be a major growth accelerator.

My wife and I do a "Couples QBR" over dinner every ninety days.

We bring notes, a bottle of wine, and our truth.

We cover the following:

- What's working in our marriage?
- What's not?
- What are we building together this quarter?

We've set goals like:

- Three date nights per month
- Save $100K toward the Scottsdale house
- Replace the damn appliances

We treat our relationship like a startup—one that deserves strategy, investment, and heart.

Why Quarterly Reviews Work

They keep you honest.

You stop rewriting the logbook and start owning the results. They keep you agile. If something's not working, you pivot fast—before the year's gone. They build compound momentum.

One solid quarter is good. Two is transformation. Four? That's a whole new life.

The Lesson My Dad Never Learned

My dad was brilliant at reacting. But he never stopped moving long enough to reflect.

That's the difference between surviving and succeeding. Survivors drive until the tank's empty.

Executives pull over, check the gauges, refuel, and get back on the road with purpose.

Reflection Prompt

Your next QBR starts now.

Grab a notebook and answer:

"If I were the CEO of my own life, how would I rate this past quarter—and what would I do differently next quarter?"

Be honest. Brutal if you must.

Then schedule your next ninety-day review before you close the notebook.

Because hope isn't a strategy. And neither is winging it.

STOP AND REFLECT

If you were the CEO of You Inc., how would you grade your last quarter—in health, wealth, relationships, and growth?

Where's your red, yellow, and green?

What are the three most important outcomes you want to achieve in the next ninety days?

Can you define what *success* looks like for each—in one sentence?

Running your life like a business will change everything—your focus, your momentum, your results. But here's the part no one talks about:

If you don't step away, the system will eventually eat you alive.

Quarterly discipline is powerful, but it has a dark side. When you're pushing, tracking, measuring, optimizing, improving... you can forget the one metric that actually keeps you human: Stillness.

I learned the hard way that even the best-designed life will pull you into burnout if you never shut it all down. You can only operate at max output for so long before your body, your mind, or your relationships start waving the white flag.

And the truth is, most people try to think their way out of exhaustion.

You can't. You have to *walk* your way out—into silence, into nature, into a place where the noise can't follow you.

Every quarter needs a finish line. And every finish line needs a reset.

For me, that reset isn't a spa day or a long weekend. It's a mountain. A storm. A pack on my back and nothing but altitude and silence ahead of me.

Because the only way to hear your own voice again is to get far enough away that the world stops shouting in your ear.

And that brings us to one of the most important lessons in this entire book—a lesson that doesn't come from boardrooms, balance sheets, or strategic planning…

…but from a lightning strike, a backpack, and the smell of burning pines.

CHAPTER 16
THE SMELL OF BURNING PINES

The 72-Hour Effect and Why You Need to Step Away to
Find Yourself Again

Boom!

A bolt of lightning struck a hundred-foot pine less than a hundred yards to my left. The top exploded into flames, bark flying in fist-sized chunks as the electricity ripped its way down to the ground.

If not for the driving downpour, I might've worried about wildfire—but the rain snuffed the flames as fast as they appeared. I crouched low, forty-four pounds of gear balanced on my back, breath quickening as the air filled with that unmistakable scent: burning pine and ozone.

"Holy shit, that was really close! Did you see that?" yelled Dave—our rookie for the year, the "add-a-man." His first time on our annual backpacking trip. I'd like to tell you that kind of thing was unusual, but it's become our Day One tradition: chaos by nature.

For whatever reason, for several years in a row now, our annual backpacking trip starts out by staring death in the face. We try to plan for weather, we try to plan for everything, but the mountain never seems to care about our plans.

"Spread out!" I shouted, as our column bunched up on the trail. "Ten feet apart! If we take a hit, I'd rather have seven guys doing CPR on one than one guy trying to pick who to save."

Dave stared back, half-laughing, half-terrified. "Wait, are you serious right now?"

I didn't answer. The sky cracked again, and we moved—each man his own small, trembling island—as we ascended into the cloud that swallowed Pike's Peak.

We were past the point of no return, and there was nothing to do now but climb.

When we'd get home a few days later, we'd find out from our wives that a rare tornado was spinning just a mile or so to our right during our climb, knocking down pine trees and chewing a path through the foliage.

The Mountain's Terms

The higher we climbed, the colder it got. Ninety degrees at the base in Manitou Springs, now low forties and falling fast. Hail the size of grapes hammered our bodies, leaving welts that would last days.

Thunder rolled over us in waves. The believers prayed. The nonbelievers asked them to throw in a good word for their friends. We all laughed nervously, because there was nothing else to do, nowhere to hide.

It was July 20, 2023—our annual backpacking trip. And come hell or high water (and there was plenty of both), we were getting to camp at a spot I had designated for us, halfway up the mountain.

It is a spot we dubbed "Carl's Cavern," which is a granite outcrop big enough to fit ten people under, near a meadow and a babbling creek. It had everything we needed to survive the night—we just had to get there in one piece.

Steak Night and Sanity

Our first night ritual never changes: steak and baked potatoes by the fire. Every guy carries his own frozen ribeye in the pack—thawed by the time we hit camp. By dusk, we were smoke covered, laughing, chewing like wolves, and feeling that unmistakable shift: the first exhale of freedom.

This is when the flasks of bourbon and red wine emerge from backpacks, and the discomfort involved in getting there falls away as the moon rises, and we sink into our ultralight camp chairs around a roaring campfire.

No Wi-Fi. No Slack pings. No texts from work. Just pine smoke, steak fat, Bigfoot stories, and laughter echoing off granite walls.

And sometimes—pure stupidity and hilarity.

Everyone Becomes an Idiot After 10,000 Feet

You put a group of grown men in the mountains long enough and eventually evolution breaks down. We devolve. Something in our DNA says, *"We're animals again—let's act like it."*

Take my friend Rudy, for example.

One year he dug himself a perfect backcountry latrine—deep hole, stable tree nearby, textbook execution. He dropped his pants to his ankles, grabbed the tree trunk with both hands, and carefully leaned back over the hole like a man performing a delicate ballet move.

And somehow—God only knows how—he still managed to accidentally dump directly into his own pants.

He stared at them with this mix of betrayal and disbelief, like the pants had personally failed him. Then, with no other option, he buried them. Right there. Deep in the Colorado mountains. A nylon time capsule of shame.

The next year, our friend Rob declared he would *never* repeat Rudy's mistake.

His solution?

Get completely naked.

Strip down to factory settings. Remove all risk variables.

So, deep in the woods—miles from camp, convinced not a single human soul had passed through in days—he disrobed, felt the sun on his skin, and squatted over another expertly dug hole.

Right then—at the precise moment he reached full vulnerability— *an entire troop of Cub Scouts* rounded the bend in the trail.

There he stood, eyes squeezed shut, both hands covering his privates like he was trying to block a solar eclipse.

The Cub Scouts marched past him in absolute silence, pretending harder than they had ever pretended in their young lives not to see the naked man in the woods.

When he came back to camp, he didn't speak for a full hour.

These are the moments that only happen in nature—when the wild resets you, humbles you, and reminds you that civilization is just a very thin layer of paint.

The Seventy-Two Hour Effect

Scientists have written about it. Navy SEALs and wilderness therapists swear by it.

Spend seventy-two hours off the grid, immersed in nature, and your nervous system rewires itself.

Day one, you're twitchy. You reach for your phone that isn't there. You wonder what's happening in the inbox you swore you'd stop checking.

Day two, your brain starts to defrag. Thoughts slow down. Sleep returns. Food tastes different. Ice-cold water filtered from mountain streams becomes the best thing you've ever tasted.

By day three, something ancient wakes up. The static in your head fades, replaced by the rhythm of wind, breath, and heartbeat.

That's the seventy-two hour effect. Your body remembering what "normal" actually feels like.

Why You Have to Step Away

If you're running your life on quarters, you need a reset between them. A real one. Not a long weekend with your laptop. Not a family trip with a packed itinerary.

A solo shutdown.

Three days, no email, no phone, no notifications. Just you, your thoughts, and the sound of trees talking to the wind.

Because here's the truth:

Reflection doesn't happen in noise. It happens in silence.

You can't hear your inner compass if it's drowned out by phone alerts.

The woods strip away the false urgency. After a few days out there, you realize how much of your "busy" is self-inflicted. How you aren't being missed at work as much as you think you are.

You start to breathe again. You start to think again. And if you stay long enough, you start to *feel* again.

How to Run Your Own 72-Hour Reset

You don't need to climb Pike's Peak—or dodge lightning—to get there. But you do need to make it sacred.

1. Leave the phone.

Airplane mode isn't enough. Power it off and bury it in your pack. Tell people you're unreachable.

2. Go alone or with the right few.

No drama, no distractions, no chatter about work. Choose people who know how to embrace the calm.

3. Pack simple.

Shelter. Warmth. Water. Food. When your gear list is short, your attention expands.

4. Let the woods recalibrate you.

You'll fight it the first day. You'll start surrendering on the second. By the third, you'll wonder why you ever needed a phone to feel alive.

The Spiritual Return on Investment

Every time I step off a mountain after one of these trips, I feel like someone wiped my hard drive clean and reinstalled only what matters. My wife says it's like a different man comes home.

The chatter quiets. The priorities reorder themselves.

The stress that once felt inescapable starts to feel optional.

And that's the real point of running your life in quarters:

You push hard. You measure. You grind.

Then you *unplug*. You *reset*. You let the system breathe.

No business can run at 100 percent utilization forever. Neither can you.

The Smell That Stays

The next morning, the storm was gone. Steam rose from the soaked forest floor. Every breath smelled like wet pine and earth and freedom.

That smell—the smell of burning pines—stayed with me long after the trip ended.

It's the smell of surrender.

Of coming back to yourself.

Every summer, I chase that smell again.

Not to escape the world, but to remember how to live in it.

STOP AND REFLECT

When was the last time you truly unplugged—no phone, no agenda, no plan to capture content?

What in your life feels urgent… but isn't as important as you might think?

What would happen if you stopped answering every alert and started listening to silence instead?

When was the last time you went seventy-two hours without checking a screen, a message, or a metric?

There's something dangerous that happens when you step off a mountain and back into the real world.

Your brain turns back on. Your instincts sharpen. Your bullshit tolerance drops to zero.

After seventy-two hours in the wild, you stop mistaking urgency for importance. You stop letting Slack dictate your self-worth. You stop believing the corporate fairy tale that "hard work speaks for itself."

Because once you've stared down lightning at 12,000 feet, you realize something simple and brutal:

Nobody is coming to hand you the life you want—not in the woods, and sure as hell not at work.

Those three days off-grid strip you down to the truth:

Your job is not your identity. Your employer is not your family. And your paycheck is not the ceiling of your potential—it's the fuel for your freedom.

Coming down that mountain, you start to see the game clearly again. Work is simply a wealth creation vehicle. Think of it like a big growing pie. And every quarter is another chance to take a bigger slice—or walk away hungry.

So, wipe the pine smoke off your jacket. Step back into the arena. Because now that your head's clear, it's time for you to do what most people never do: Claim your piece of the pie.

CHAPTER 17
GET YOUR SLICE OF THE PIE AT WORK

Because no one's going to hand you wealth—you've got to claim your piece.

The first breath back from the woods always smells different.

Pine, asphalt, and ambition.

You've just spent three days unplugged—no phone, no Wi-Fi, no noise.

Now you're back in civilization, showered, caffeinated, and staring at the Monday inbox.

Here's the shift that happens after seventy-two hours off the grid:

You stop reacting. You start seeing.

And what you'll notice, once the static fades, is this:

Your W-2 income is only one of your income streams. But it's the engine that funds every other one.

If you work in tech, you are in one of the most opportunity-rich ecosystems on the planet.

You can build wealth faster here—if you treat your career like a business and your employer like your first investor.

1. Think Like a Portfolio, Not a Paycheck

Your salary isn't security. It's capital—fuel for building the life you want.

Your 401(k), bonuses, RSUs (restricted stock units), and side ventures are all revenue streams.

But the W-2? That's your cornerstone.

Maximize it. Squeeze every ounce of learning, network, and equity out of it.

Don't coast through a six-figure role like it's a salary; run it like it's a startup with one client—you.

The question isn't "What do I earn?"

It's "How much leverage can I create with what I earn?"

2. Attach to the Right People

In the software business, proximity equals profit. The right relationships can compress a five-year career curve into one. I've seen it happen.

Find the people who make money move—the executives who close, the CSMs who retain, the PMs who deliver, the leaders who inspire. Get in their orbit.

Attach yourself to high-impact projects where visibility is high and results are measurable.

You'll learn faster, grow faster, and earn faster.

The last thing you want is to work on the easy projects. Stretch yourself and reach for more than you think you're capable of.

The rule of thumb: Get closer to big outcomes, or big problems, not comfort.

3. Align With the Right Clients

All clients are not created equal. Some are small logos with loud opinions; others are quiet giants who make or break your fiscal year. Some could be small logos that could become giants, if played right.

If you can deliver outcomes for the giants—the Amazons, Deloittes, Walmarts, Exxons of your world—you'll never struggle for leverage again. Same goes for if you can show a track record of being able to catapult small clients to exponential growth.

Because when your name becomes synonymous with results, the brand that benefits most is yours. And once you have built a solid brand, nobody can take that away from you.

That's how raises happen quietly. That's how stock grants show up without your begging for them. That's how leaders start sentences with your name when big opportunities surface.

4. Measure Your Impact Like a QBR

Your quarterly business review doesn't just belong to your customers—it belongs to you.

Every ninety days, run your own Career QBR.

Ask yourself:

- What did I commit to deliver this quarter?
- What outcomes did I actually produce?
- What measurable value did those outcomes drive?
- Who noticed?

Turn those answers into a one-page "success slide."

Use it when promotion time comes, or when you're negotiating comp. You're not just an employee—you're a business unit reporting ROI (return on investment).

5. Make Yourself a Profit Center

The highest-paid people in software aren't always in sales.

They're the ones who can connect their daily work to the company's bottom line.

Whether you're in Product, Success, Marketing, or Ops—learn the language of money:

Revenue. Margin. Retention. Expansion.

Tie your metrics to those outcomes and speak in business cases, not activity logs. When you can say, "My initiative helped renew $5M in ARR," you stop being overhead and start being investment.

6. Build While You Earn

Maximizing your W-2 is step one.

But don't stop there.

Use the stability it gives you to fund your next streams:

- A small rental property.
- A furniture flipping business.
- An advisory side gig.
- A content brand that monetizes your expertise.
- A niche SaaS (software as a service) play you can grow quietly on weekends.

Your day job feeds your dream job—if you play it right.

7. Don't Wait for Permission

Companies love to say, "We're a family."

But families don't lay you off in Q4, when the shit hits the fan.

So, build your value in daylight, not desperation. Ask for raises while you're winning, not while you're worried. Negotiate equity before it's fashionable. And if you outgrow your environment, move. Quickly.

Loyalty is admirable; leverage is wealth.

8. Help Make the Pie Bigger

Here's the part most people miss:

If you want a bigger slice, make the pie bigger.

Drive outcomes. Drive adoption. Drive retention. Drive revenue.

Be the person who lifts the whole system, not just the self.

When you create undeniable impact, leaders don't argue your worth—they protect it.

The Post-Hike Perspective

Many of us were raised to believe that talking about money, or the pursuit of it, is a dirty subject only to be whispered about quietly when the coast is clear. The truth is, money is simply a tool to amplify the parts of our lives that we enjoy, and turn the volume down on the parts that we don't.

When I'm deep in the mountains, unplugged from everything that buzzes and pings, I remember what really matters: time, health, freedom.

Money is just the tool that buys more of those.

So, when I come back to work, I treat my job like a funding round for the next adventure.

I give it focus. Intensity. Precision.

Because every quarter is another chance to grow wealth, reputation, and autonomy—if you're deliberate about it.

STOP AND REFLECT

If your job disappeared tomorrow, what would still pay you? And if the answer is "nothing yet," then ask yourself:

"How can I maximize my W-2 today to seed everything that comes next?"

Your income isn't the destination—it's the engine. Tune it, fuel it, and drive it like you're building something bigger than a paycheck.

Here's the thing nobody tells you about getting your slice of the pie at work:

Once you've carved out your piece—once you finally start earning real money, real influence, real leverage, you're not done. You're barely getting warmed up.

Because the corporate world will happily hand you a title, a raise, a round of applause…

and then stand back to see if you burn out, blow up, or walk away over something stupid.

Most people do.

They get their first big win and start believing the universe owes them an easier ride. They get offended, impatient, bored, or entitled. They forget that getting ahead and staying ahead are two completely different games.

The climb to the top of the pie chart feels sexy. Staying there feels like work.

That's where the amateurs tap out. And that's where the true pros separate themselves.

Because wealth isn't built in the victory laps. Reputation isn't built in the highlight reel. Legacy isn't built in the quarters—it's built in the years.

Once you've claimed your slice, the real questions become:

Can you keep showing up long after the novelty wears off?

Can you stay steady when the spotlight moves on?

Can you keep playing the game when the game stops feeling fun?

Success favors the stubborn. The patient. The ones who don't quit the table when they take a bad beat. And that brings us straight into the next chapter—a chapter about the single trait that has made more millionaires than luck, talent, or timing ever have:

The long game.

CHAPTER 18
PLAY THE LONG GAME

Because greatness isn't found in the sprint, it's built in the seasons.

Somewhere out there, on the road, I realized life rewards the persistent far more than it does the gifted.

Show me a great talent, and I'll show you someone who's likely to flame out when the applause fades or the challenge changes. Show me a great genius, and I'll show you someone who will probably get frustrated with management, quit over a minor slight, or self-destruct when they feel underappreciated.

Playing the long game is something everyone talks about—but very few actually do.

Because it's not glamorous. It's not exciting. It's about sticking with something. Taking total ownership—and keeping it—over an extended period of time.

The long game is about being known as "Clutch," or "The Guy."

The one who always has it under control. The one who always delivers. The one who doesn't panic when things go sideways.

And here's the quiet, uncomfortable truth: If you do it long enough, your leaders, peers, and even clients will start to take you for granted. They'll stop noticing the miracles you pull off. Because you make it look easy. That's the cost of mastery: The better you get, the more invisible your effort becomes.

But that's also what separates professionals from performers. Performers crave recognition. Professionals grind out results.

When I think about pride, patience, and the cost of walking away too soon, I can't help but think about my dad.

In 1976, the Vietnam War had just come to an abrupt and uneasy close. After years of living on the edge of the world, he found himself grounded—stationed in Austin, Texas, supervising the landscaping crews at Bergstrom Air Force Base.

It was a jarring change. Only months before, he had been part of one of the most dangerous and impactful secretive assignments imaginable: working with MAC-V-SOG on missions to rescue our POWs in the jungles of Vietnam.

When the war ended, America left behind too many of its own: Men who were missing in action or presumed captured. That haunted him for the rest of his life. He felt like his country—and maybe even his purpose—had just walked away and left those men behind.

One afternoon, a major at Bergstrom made a snide remark about the cut of one of the lawns his crew was managing. Something small. Something unimportant in the big picture. But to a man who had risked his life for others, that criticism cut deep.

He snapped. After a bitter argument, he marched straight into the office and submitted his retirement papers that very day.

His colonel called him personally, told him he was next in line for a big promotion to Chief Master Sergeant. That it came with a transfer to Washington, DC, and a seat at the table shaping the next generation of military strategy. But his pride got the better of him.

He walked away. Just like that, his twenty-two-year career was over.

For years, he regretted that decision. He started managing the motel full time after that and eventually built a trucking company from scratch, but he always carried that weight. It taught me something that's stuck with me my entire life: Pride kills more futures than failure ever will.

The long game requires patience. It demands humility. Sometimes you've got to eat shit sandwiches, and look like you enjoy them, to get to the champagne and caviar part of your life.

You must be willing to stay the course even when it feels beneath you because sometimes the mission isn't glamorous, but it's still yours.

Over the years, I've watched talented people come and go—some brilliant, some burned out, some simply bored. I've seen the "new hotshot" get promoted before they ever faced a real crisis, only to crumble when things didn't go according to plan. And I've seen the quiet grinders—the ones who showed up every day, kept their promises, and didn't make excuses—build careers that spanned decades and families that stood the test of time.

Persistence is the great equalizer.

It's what turns ordinary people into extraordinary ones. It's what separates the short-term flash from the long-term fire.

In the software world, it's easy to get seduced by velocity—quarterly goals, annual bonuses, stock refreshers, promotions. But the real players? They are the ones still standing twenty years later. They play a different game entirely. They know consistency compounds faster than charisma.

Playing the long game means learning to live in the boring middle. It's staying focused after the honeymoon phase ends. It's showing up when the dopamine wears off. It's holding the line when everyone else starts cutting corners.

The long game requires a kind of patience that can't be faked. You need to get comfortable being overlooked, under-credited, and occasionally disrespected while still performing at the same high standard. You need to find your pride not in being praised, but in knowing you're the reason the whole thing didn't fall apart.

It's not easy, but it's what separates those who make a splash from those who leave a legacy.

You see it in professional sports. Talent gets you drafted, but persistence builds dynasties. The greats stay in the gym after everyone else goes home. They take care of their bodies, their minds, their relationships. They play hurt, they play tired, and they play for the love of the game.

Entrepreneurs have it too. They weather downturns, investor drama, and sleepless nights.

They survive on grit and coffee when inspiration runs dry. They keep showing up because they can't imagine doing anything else.

That's what the long game is about—ownership. Not temporary enthusiasm. Not flashes of brilliance. Ownership.

You take responsibility for your domain—every client, every deliverable, every promise—and you keep it. You keep it so long, and with such quiet confidence, that the entire organization leans on you without realizing it. And when they finally do—when they see how much you've carried—*that's* when the respect comes. Not from what you say, but from what you sustain.

When I think about my dad walking away that day, I can't help but wonder how many times in my own life I've come close to doing the same thing, letting pride, exhaustion, or frustration get the best of me.

Because the truth is, playing the long game isn't just about staying in the fight, it's about knowing which fights to stay in. There are seasons where you have to double down and grind through the pain, and others where walking away isn't quitting, it's strategy.

That's where the real challenge lies.

I've always brought a high level of intensity to my work. It's my default gear.

But that intensity comes with a cost. Burnout doesn't announce itself; it sneaks up on you in small ways. You start sleeping less, snapping quicker, losing the spark you once had. And one day you realize that what used to light you up now just drains you.

That's the edge of the long game—knowing how to keep your fire burning without burning yourself down.

In poker terms, it's learning when to fold your losing cards and when to hang in and play for the river. You can't win every hand, but you can stay at the table long enough to play the ones that matter.

In my own career, I've noticed a pattern. When the company's winning, when there's energy in the air, when growth feels inevitable, I'm at my best. I go all in. I pour everything I've got into the mission. But when that momentum starts to slow, when leadership gets complacent, or innovation stalls, or the vision starts to drift, that's when the alarm bells go off. That's when I start quietly looking at my cards and thinking about the next table.

That doesn't come from fear or disloyalty—it comes from learning the lesson my dad never got to apply.

He let his pride decide for him. I've tried to let persistence and timing do the talking instead.

Because if you want to play the long game, you have to know the difference between quitting and moving on. Between pride and patience. Between ego and endurance.

And that's what this whole thing really comes down to:

Learning how to stay when it's worth it, and knowing how to walk when it's not.

Persistence wins the long game, but wisdom decides which game you keep playing.

Success Planning Takeaways

- Play for seasons, not moments. Consistency compounds—every month of doing the right thing builds a foundation that talent alone can't match.

- Master emotional endurance. Learn to operate at 90 percent even on your worst days—that's how professionals separate from performers.
- Be patient, not passive. Sticking around doesn't mean standing still; it means improving your position every single day.
- Check your pride. Don't make permanent decisions out of temporary emotions.
- Know when to move. Learn the difference between persistence and stagnation because sometimes the long game means changing tables, not quitting the game.

Because sometimes, playing the long game means knowing exactly when it's time to cut the rope.

STOP
AND
REFLECT

When was the last time pride, ego, or frustration tempted you to walk away from something worth finishing?

What would have happened if you'd stayed the course a little longer?

How well do you perform when nobody's watching—when the praise stops, when the project drags, when the energy dips?

The thing about playing the long game is, if you stay in it long enough, you eventually learn that endurance isn't just about holding on. It's about knowing *what to let go of.*

Most people don't fail because they lack grit. They fail because they waste their grit on the wrong people, the wrong problems, the wrong mountains.

And sometimes the toughest part of the long game isn't patience, or humility, or persistence.

It's recognizing when the climb you're on is no longer your climb... and when the thing you're gripping so tightly is the very thing keeping you from going any higher.

Playing the long game teaches you loyalty. Wisdom teaches you limits. Because there comes a moment in every journey—career, relationship, family, life—when you're forced to confront a brutal truth:

You can't summit with a rope that's pulling you down.

That's the moment that separates the people who last from the people who don't. The moment where pride won't save you, and patience won't save you, and grit won't save you.

Only one thing will:

The courage to cut the rope.

CHAPTER 19
CUT THE ROPE

Because sometimes holding on costs more than letting go.

Early in my career at HP, I shared a cubical with a guy named Michael Keen.

On paper, he was just another engineer. In reality, he was one of the most unexpectedly profound mentors I've ever met.

Mike had lived three different lives by the time he landed in tech. He'd been a Wall Street bond trader, an Everest climbing guide, and now—somehow—was starting a new life in tech as an engineer, just like me, only twenty years older.

He was full of wild stories. Outrageous. Hilarious. Heartbreaking. But one of them changed how I see life forever.

The Man in the Crevasse

He told me about a climb on Everest—one of those brutal expeditions that tests everything you believe about yourself and takes everything you've got.

He and his team were roped together, navigating a stretch of ice that looked stable until it wasn't. One of the climbers slipped and fell into a crevasse—wedged deep, cold, and screaming for help.

They tried everything. Ropes. Pulleys. Anchors. For hours.

The sun was falling. The temperature plummeting. Every minute they stayed increased the odds that all of them would die.

Finally, the lead climber gave the order. They cut the rope.

Mike said it flatly, no bravado, no drama. Just truth. It haunted him—but it saved the rest of the team.

"Cut the rope, bro."

From that day on, anytime I was buried in a doomed project or stuck trying to fix something that no longer served me, Mike would look over and say:

"Cut the rope, bro."

It became a mantra. So much so, that it became burned in my brain.

I'd hear it every time I was pouring energy into something—or someone—that wasn't giving anything back.

Cut the rope.

Let go of the client who will never renew, the friend who keeps you small, the family member who only calls to criticize, and the relationship that costs your peace.

Cutting the rope isn't cruelty. It's clarity.

You Can't Climb Higher Carrying Dead Weight

We love to talk about "holding on."

To people. To jobs. To comfort. To history. But not everything—or everyone—is meant to make the full climb with you. Growth demands lightness.

Sometimes, the higher you go, the fewer people can breathe at your altitude. And that's not arrogance—it's facts.

People will say, "You've changed."

And you have. You're supposed to.

Growth looks like outgrowing the version of yourself that could tolerate certain environments, certain conversations, certain energies.

You're not abandoning people. You're refusing to die on a mountain they chose not to climb.

The 72-Hour Rule of Relationships

Remember that 72-hour effect from the woods?

Three days away from noise, and your body resets.

The same thing happens when you step back from toxic people, draining work, or relationships that no longer align.

Take seventy-two hours to unplug from anyone or anything that's been clouding your head. No texts. No calls. No emotional debates.

You'll be shocked how different it feels when the static clears. How much lighter you are when you stop trying to fix people who don't want to grow.

Keep What Feeds You

Life's too short to keep things that steal your oxygen.

Keep what gives you energy:

- People who root for your growth.
- Work that excites you.
- Environments that bring out your best self.

And release what drains you:

- Obligations built on guilt.
- Conversations that always end in circles.
- Dreams that used to fit but don't anymore.

This isn't selfish—it's survival. You can't pour into others from an empty tank. You can't mentor, build, or lead if you're clinging to something pulling you down.

Loyalty Has a Shelf Life

Loyalty is beautiful—until it becomes self-destruction.

Being loyal to a person, a company, or even a dream that's stopped evolving isn't noble. It's expensive.

When loyalty stops being mutual, it turns into bondage. When growth becomes guilt, it's time to reevaluate the rope. You can love people deeply and still recognize when they're not meant to continue the climb.

The Hardest Rope I Ever Cut

There's one rope I wish I'd never *had* to cut. My mom.

When I was a kid, she was pure light—she was the party. Her house was spotless, her laugh contagious, and every July 4th she made us feel like our house was THE place to be for her legendary multi-day Independence Day parties, complete with barbequed brisket and where anyone was welcome. She made everything so much fun.

But somewhere along the way, the light dimmed.

It started slowly—too many drinks, a few bad nights, the kind of things families quietly excuse. Then my dad died. And the silence swallowed her whole. A back injury she got lifting my dad in and out of bed led to pain pills. The pain pills led to harder drugs. And before long, she was drinking a liter of tequila a day and using heroin just to feel okay.

I was stunned when I found out. If you knew my mother, you'd be stunned too. She was the last person you'd ever expect to go down that road. I grew up in a strictly anti-drug household, the kind where even casual talk of drugs was off-limits, so the idea that my own mother could not only try but become dependent on something as destructive as heroin felt impossible. But addiction doesn't care who you are or what you believe. I've since learned that opioid dependency is one of the most devastating epidemics in America, destroying millions of lives like hers, not always through death, but through the quiet ruin of finances, careers, relationships, and the will to keep going.

The last year of her life was one long slow painful goodbye, that I still struggle with today. She spent every penny my dad had left behind on drugs and alcohol, then ran up another $70k in credit card debt, on her way out. I rarely heard from her, except the occasional call to try to convince me to send her money. When I refused and suggested she check herself into rehab she'd explode in anger and hang up on me. Sometimes I wouldn't hear from her again for months.

As the wheels came off, the neighbors started calling. Another ambulance. Another ER trip. Another night where she refused to let me in, refused to let me speak with her doctors. The house that once hosted laughter and love now smelled of rot and regret. The woman who had once held our world together was now slipping into one she couldn't climb out of.

I tried everything—calls, visits, offers to move her closer. But she didn't want help.

And the hardest truth I've ever had to face is that you can't save someone who doesn't want to be saved.

The last time I spoke with her, I knew it was over. She called after a lengthy hospital stay, her body beginning to fail from the effects of her lifestyle. Something inside me snapped. Years of frustration, fear, and heartbreak came pouring out. I told her exactly how I saw it, how she had burned through everything Dad had worked so hard to leave her, how she was in danger of losing the house, how disappointed and disgusted I was by the way she was spending her last bit of time on this Earth. She wasn't even opening her mail anymore to look at the bills. Finally, I quoted Mom back to herself, something she had taught me as a child: "The lord helps those who help themselves, remember you taught me that?"

She got quiet, she almost sounded apologetic, like she knew she had done terrible wrongs that could never be made right. She was embarrassed of her behavior. Then the call ended.

I carried guilt for years. Hell, I still carry it.

She never called again. A few months later, she was gone—estranged from family, neighbors, and friends, surrounded by others fighting the same demons, just fellow travelers she had met somewhere along the way that she had invited into her home. It sounded like such a cold, lonely way to die.

When my half brother called, I braced for bad news. And when he told me she was gone, part of me broke—but another part finally understood what Mike meant back at HP:

Sometimes holding on can be lethal.

Cutting that rope didn't mean I stopped loving her. It meant I stopped dying *with* her. It meant I finally accepted that compassion doesn't mean self-destruction.

I had to make peace with the fact that it wasn't my fault. That's the part no one talks about—that letting go of someone you love can be an act of grace, not abandonment.

Cutting the Rope Is an Act of Faith

Cutting the rope doesn't mean giving up. It means trusting that there's something ahead worth reaching for—something that requires both hands free.

Every time I've had the courage to let go, I've found new strength, new clarity, new people waiting higher up the mountain.

And every time I didn't—I got dragged into the crevasse with who or what I was trying to save.

STOP AND REFLECT

Ask Yourself:

Who or what am I still holding onto that's keeping me from climbing?

If it's not feeding your energy, your purpose, or your peace—cut the rope.

Because when you finally do, something amazing happens:

You don't fall. You rise.

Cutting the rope teaches you something nobody ever prepares you for:

Once you finally let go of the things that drain you, you're left face-to-face with the things worth holding onto.

When you strip out the noise, the chaos, the one-sided relationships, and the emotional quicksand, what's left is the real work—the people who matter, the responsibilities that shape you, and the systems that keep your life upright when everything else is shaking.

Letting go isn't the end of the story. It's the clearing.

And in that clearing, you suddenly see the truth:

If you don't create alignment at home, you'll never have alignment anywhere. If you can't manage the expectations of the people you love, you'll never manage the expectations of the people who pay you. If you don't communicate intentionally with your own family, the boardroom won't save you.

Cutting the rope frees your hands. What you do with them next is what builds a life.

And for me, the next step was realizing this:

If I can manage million-dollar stakeholders at work, I sure as hell can manage the ones sleeping under my own roof.

Alright—let's talk about stakeholder management... the life version.

CHAPTER 20
STAKEHOLDER MANAGEMENT IN LIFE AND WORK

Because even your five-year-old can be part of the plan—if you invite them in.

In enterprise software, I manage a $50M client portfolio. Dozens of stakeholders. Competing objectives. Constant alignment.

My job isn't just to keep them satisfied, it's to keep them moving in the same direction. Every meeting, every outcome, every dollar earned depends on how well people understand their roles, expectations, and purpose.

For years, I thought that kind of coordination was reserved for boardrooms and billion-dollar clients. Then I realized: If I can manage a $50M portfolio, I can manage a family.

Because your home life deserves the same intentionality as your work life. In fact, it needs more.

Raising Twins Was My First MBA in Stakeholder Management

From the day my daughters were born, I knew one thing: treating them exactly the same would fail spectacularly.

They are individuals, but also twins. The bond they share is closer than anything I've seen on this Earth, and yet they are both such unique, amazing young women.

From the start, whether we liked it or not, they were destined to be compared, confused, and clumped together by the world.

So, I did what any self-respecting program manager would do: I made it a strategy.

We created micro-competitions:

- Who could stack blocks the fastest?
- Who could memorize their ABCs first?
- Who could finish the worksheets I'd leave out before breakfast the fastest?

Yes, those worksheets were a survival tactic. I was just trying to get an extra hour of sleep while they did "homework" with Pop-Tarts. But over time, something clicked.

They learned how to compete with love. How to strive without resentment. How to earn things instead of expecting them. How to resolve disputes between themselves.

When they wanted money, there was always work to do: paint the fence, wash the windows, dust the baseboards. Nothing was free. Nothing was given. The world waiting for them wasn't going to be kind, and I wanted them to be ready.

That edge stayed with them. Now they're grown; they are college grads on opposite coasts, thriving, independent, and accountable. That didn't happen by accident. That was culture, kicked off before breakfast, every morning.

The First Family Meeting

When they were about six, we held our first official family meeting.

I didn't know what to expect.

I just treated it like a stakeholder review.

"What's working?"

"What's not?"

"What would make this family better?"

Their answers?

- "More hamburger nights."
- "More game nights."
- "Popcorn with gummy bears during movies."

It was funny, but it was real. They felt heard because they were invited in.

Even little kids crave structure and ownership, and they just need a seat at the table.

We kept holding those meetings. We added Special Days—one twin with Mom, one with Dad—so each got individual attention. No competition. No noise. Just connection.

It wasn't chaos. It was culture, evolving through communication and lots of love.

Marriage as a Board of Directors

Most couples try to wing it.

They'd never run a business that way, but they run their marriage like a startup without a strategy. My wife and I started holding monthly financial meetings early in our marriage. No surprises. No hidden spending. No guilt.

We reviewed such things as:

- Budget performance
- Upcoming expenses
- Savings and investments
- Areas to tighten

- Places we can relax and reward ourselves

It's not about money; it's about alignment.

We don't just cohabitate.

We co-build.

Track Your Net Worth Like a CFO

Every month—on the first—pay every bill and update our net worth dashboard.

Yes, it's a spreadsheet. Yes, it's old school. And yes, it works.

I track the following:

- Cash and checking balances
- Investments and retirement accounts
- Property values and mortgage balances
- Liabilities, down to the last cent
- Spending, broken down by credit card

Then I graph it. Watch the slope. See the compound effect.

Nothing motivates a couple more than watching their collective effort turn into measurable progress. It's not about greed. It's about accountability. The scoreboard creates ownership, and the charts help us see into the future.

Run Your Home Like a High-Trust Company

When I run client accounts, I focus on three pillars:

1. Clarity—Everyone knows the mission.
2. Ownership—Everyone knows their role.
3. Cadence—Everyone knows when we're checking in again.

Turns out, that's exactly what makes a family work, too.

Want fewer arguments? Set expectations early. Want better engagement? Create feedback loops. Want consistent momentum? Schedule it.

Meetings, one-on-ones, offsites—they're not corporate jargon. They're communication rituals.

And when you apply them at home, life gets smoother.

You're the CEO, but Not the Only Shareholder

Being the CEO of your family doesn't mean control. It means stewardship.

You don't dictate. You align. You don't command. You coordinate.

Every person under your roof—spouse, child, even pet—is a stakeholder in the mission.

They have emotional equity in the outcome.

So, treat them like investors:

- Give visibility into what's happening.
- Celebrate the wins.
- Talk about the misses.
- Adjust the roadmap together.

When everyone feels seen, valued, and part of the process, loyalty skyrockets.

Culture by Design, Not Default

A family, just like a company, develops culture—whether you build it intentionally or not.

If you don't define it, entropy will. If you don't communicate it, resentment will.

So be deliberate. Make values visible. Turn traditions into operating principles.

At work, you measure Key Performance Indicators (KPIs). At home, you measure joy, trust, and progress.

That's real wealth.

STOP AND REFLECT

Ask Yourself:

Who are the three to five most important stakeholders in your life right now?

And what systems—meetings, check-ins, dashboards, or shared rituals—are you using to stay aligned?

If your family, team, or inner circle were a company—how aligned would you be right now?

Does everyone know the mission, their role, and when the next check-in is?

Are you managing your household like a boss or leading it like a visionary?

What shift would make your "company of family" stronger over the next quarter?

Once you start running your life like a real portfolio of stakeholders—spouse, kids, career, health, money—you realize something important:

Systems are easy to love when things are calm. You find out what they're really worth when the storm hits.

Family meetings, shared dashboards, money talks, clear roles, open communication—those aren't just "nice to have." They're your lifeboats.

It's one thing to align your household when everyone's busy, the economy's humming, and the calendar's full of sports, travel, and school events.

It's another thing entirely when the world slams on the brakes. When the office goes dark. When the kids are home twenty-four-seven. When the headlines are all fear, and nobody knows what tomorrow looks like.

That's when you find out if your "culture by design" is real—or just something you talked about between Netflix episodes.

For us, that test showed up in 2020.

The world went into lockdown. Most people waited to see what would happen next.

We decided to build who we were going to be on the other side.

CHAPTER 21
STRONGER THAN BEFORE

Because when the world paused, we pressed go.

In 2020, the world stopped. Airports went quiet. Offices emptied. Schools shut down. For the first time in our lives, we weren't just working from home, we were stuck there.

It was a global pause. And everyone had to decide who they were going to be when it ended.

Some froze. Some waited for permission to live again. Some broke down. It may sound crazy, but I have a buddy whose wife is still shopping with a mask, then washing the groceries before bringing them into the house, now six years later. Sadly, COVID broke a lot of people.

But the ones who thrived—the ones who came out of it stronger than before—were the ones who treated the downtime like a design sprint, not a death sentence.

Structure Is a Survival Skill

The same principles I used in enterprise software—stakeholder alignment, clarity of mission, cadence of accountability—became the operating system for our home life during lockdown.

The systems were already there: family meetings, shared goals, clear communication.

All we had to do was double down on them. While the world drifted into chaos, we created order. While others lost rhythm, we built new rituals.

Every family member had a role. Every day had a purpose. Every week had a win. That's what kept us sane. And successful.

The Decision That Changed Everything

Early in the pandemic, my wife and I made a deal:

We weren't going to let this moment shrink us.

If the world was going to slow down, we were going to speed up in all the right ways—health, mindset, and opportunity.

So, while the world was hoarding toilet paper and doom-scrolling through *Tiger King* memes, we were ordering a Peloton. We cleared out the basement. Built a home gym. Wrote down goals. Set up a schedule.

If we were going to be stuck inside, we were coming out stronger, fitter, sharper, and more focused than ever.

The Basement Became the Battlefield

It started with one bike. But momentum is contagious.

Soon, the basement transformed into a full-fledged performance lab:

Peloton Tread. Dumbbells. Bands. Racks. Benches. Every ride or run was accountability and therapy rolled into one.

We tracked milestones. Competed. High-fived strangers on the leaderboard. Compared notes on the various runs or rides we did that day.

The world outside was unraveling. But inside that basement, we were building something unshakable—discipline. When everything else felt uncertain, discipline became our stability.

Florida, Cabo, and the Choice to Keep Living

Not everything we built was indoors.

Once travel restrictions eased, we headed to Arizona, Florida, Texas—and later Cabo San Lucas—to reset under open skies.

Those trips weren't about escape. They were about living without fear.

Sitting on our patio in Cabo, watching the sun melt into the Pacific, I remember thinking:

"The world's in panic, but we're still moving the ball down the field. The world is afraid to travel, so that just means more beach and tacos for us."

Everyone was waiting for the world to return to normal. But we weren't willing to just sit around and wait. While some were slipping back down the hill, we were moving the rock up the hill.

That's the advantage of a success-planning mindset—you don't wait for the conditions to be perfect. You build systems that thrive in any condition.

Fitness Was Just the Framework

We didn't "find time" to work out. We *scheduled* it. We didn't "hope" to stay positive. We *designed* it. Optimism and gratitude became part of our daily ritual.

Health became our new project plan:

- Daily workouts on the shared family calendar
- Step goals tracked like KPIs

- Progress photos and milestones logged like performance reviews

We used the same structure that worked at work, and it worked at home.

Because fitness isn't about luck. It's about logistics.

Career Momentum in a Standstill

While many people were waiting for "after COVID" to make moves, I leaned in.

Remote work made visibility harder, but also easier, so I made my value louder. When states opened up again like Arizona, Florida, and Texas, I made myself very visible, as I found clients to visit there and was one of the first at my company to resume doing business face to face.

I doubled down on client outcomes, refined playbooks, and built relationships that still pay dividends today.

In enterprise software, crisis separates the order-takers from the outcome-makers. I decided to be the latter.

The result? The best years of my career came during one of the worst years in history.

Positivity Is a Strategy

Some called it toxic positivity. I called it intentional optimism.

We didn't ignore the world's pain; we just refused to live inside it. We refused to let it pull us into a crevasse, when the rope needed to be cut.

Every morning started with gratitude, every night with reflection. We asked better questions:

"What can we build today?"

"What can we improve?"

"How can we emerge stronger?"

And we did.

Our health improved. Our marriage deepened. Our financial discipline tightened. Our family culture solidified. We became the most aligned, resilient version of ourselves we'd ever been.

The Lesson: You Don't Need Permission

People love to say, "We're all in the same boat."

We weren't. We were in the same storm, but in very different boats.

Some people drifted, waiting for rescue. We hoisted our sails.

Because waiting for permission is how you stay average. Taking control of your life is how you grow stronger.

How to Thrive in Your Next Storm

1. Define the Mission.
   Don't waste a crisis. Use it to realign.
   Ask: What's the opportunity in disguise right now?
2. Build the Systems.
   Routine is resilience.
   Create structure when life feels unpredictable.
3. Protect the Energy.
   Stay around builders, not blamers.
   Your circle is your climate.
4. Celebrate the Momentum.
   Small wins compound, especially when the world's standing still.
5. Document the Lessons.
   Crisis reveals your real operating system.
   Study it. Refine it. Use it again next time.

STOP AND REFLECT

If your fitness routine were a business account, would it be profitable or running at a loss?

Are you compounding progress or spending effort without tracking return?

If the world shut down again tomorrow, would you crumble or compound?

Because resilience isn't luck.

It's design.

And when you design it intentionally in your family, your health, and your work, you stop waiting for the world to restart.

You press *go*.

Coming out of COVID, I realized something strange:

When the world hits pause, you find out exactly what you're made of—and exactly what you've forgotten.

All that discipline we built in our basement... all that gratitude... all that momentum... it only mattered because it connected back to something older. Something deeper. Something I learned long before Peloton rides and enterprise software.

COVID made a lot of people soft. It made others sharp. But for me, it mostly made things *clear*—especially what actually mattered before any of us ever had titles, comp plans, RSUs, or LinkedIn headlines.

Because resilience isn't a new skill. It's an old one. It's built out of the dirt you grew up in, the hands that raised you, and the quiet lessons you picked up long before adulthood handed you a laptop.

And every time life slaps me down—pandemic or otherwise—I end up tracing my strength back to the same place:

A truck cab. A hot summer morning. And a blue-collar man teaching his kid how to carry himself in a world that doesn't always return the favor.

The truth is, becoming stronger isn't about reinventing yourself. It's about remembering who made you strong in the first place.

Alright. Let's go back to the road, to chicken wings, diesel fumes, and one little prefab office where I learned a lesson I've never stopped carrying.

CHAPTER 22
THE EXECUTIVE RESTROOM

Because growing doesn't mean forgetting.

I was about ten years old, riding shotgun in my dad's truck somewhere in the middle of the country. The kind of endless drive where you measure distance by diner stops and fuel receipts.

Speaking of diner stops, my dad also had this hilarious, unwavering rule about food on the road: If a place served chicken wings, he was ordering them. Period. Didn't matter if we were at a truck stop in Nebraska, a bar in Tennessee, or some no-name roadhouse in the Dakotas with a neon beer sign flickering like it was powered by prayers.

He'd eaten wings in every corner of the country and considered himself a sort of long-haul connoisseur, ranking them by crispiness, heat level, and whether the cook looked like they'd lived a hard enough life to season them properly. While other truckers compared fuel mileage or axle weight, my dad compared wing quality. Weeks would go by where it felt like wings were the only thing keeping him alive, and I swear he could tell you the best plate within a hundred-mile radius of any highway exit in America. It was one of his many quiet superpowers.

We'd been on the road for weeks, and it felt like we had eaten enough chicken wings to destroy entire lineages of chickens for millennia when we found ourselves, before sunrise, hauling wall board to a construction site. When we pulled off the highway, it wasn't to a skyscraper or a warehouse, just a gravel yard stacked with pallets and pipes, a single forklift, and a prefab office with two windows and one door.

That's where I learned one of the most important lessons of my life.

"Sorry, That Restroom's for Executives Only."

My job was simple: unstrap the load, roll up the tarps, and try to keep pace with a man who could outwork anyone.

If you've ever unloaded freight from a flatbed truck, you know the grime. It's a mixture of diesel, sweat, and highway dust that stains your hands and clothes like a badge of blue-collar honor.

Looking back, I don't know why we didn't have gloves. We'd end up covered in the stuff by the end of the job and were always ready for a shower or a good wash immediately after.

After we finished the delivery, my dad and I walked over to the little building to ask if we could wash up. The man inside looked us over—two tired truckers covered in soot—and said flatly:

"Sorry. That restroom's for executives only."

I didn't know what an executive was. But I knew what rejection felt like. I felt my dad's humiliation as he tried to reason with the guy, but it was futile. I remember thinking how unnecessary it was for the man to humiliate my dad like that, right in front of his son.

We turned without another word, got back in the truck, and drove a mile down the road. My dad pulled off on a quiet stretch of highway, and we proceeded to "cool down the tires," which is trucker slang for when you have to go back and pee on the side of the road, between the tires of your trailer, because you've got no better option.

We paused behind the rig, the sun burning down on us as a cloud of dust blew past.

I looked over at him and asked,

"Dad, what's an executive?"

He wiped his hands on an old rag and said:

"It means he's an asshole."

He paused, then looked straight at me.

"Some people make a little money and forget where they came from. When you make it, don't ever be like that guy. That was uncalled for."

I didn't fully understand what he meant back then.

But I do now.

Leave It Better Than You Found It

At most stops, when we were allowed to use the restroom, my dad had this habit. After washing up, he'd take a few extra minutes to clean—wipe the sink, straighten the paper towels, sometimes even pick up trash from the floor.

I remember watching him and asking, "Why do you always do that?"

He said, "Because this is someone else's place. You have to leave it better than you found it."

He wasn't rich. He didn't have a title. But he carried himself like a man of deep dignity, someone who believed that work, any work, deserved respect.

And that every person who worked for a living, from the truck yard to the top floor, was part of the same ecosystem keeping the world turning. That lesson stuck harder than diesel grime ever did.

What Success Should Never Erase

Fast-forward a few decades—boardrooms, hotel lounges, enterprise software deals—and I still see that man behind the prefab desk every now and then. He shows up in the executives who look *through* people instead of *at* them. The ones who forget that every signature, every contract, every success story sits on the shoulders of people who get their hands dirty.

So I made myself a promise: I would never be the guy with the "executives only" sign on the door.

I'd shake hands with the janitor and the CEO with the same respect.

I'd remember the smell of that truck, the ache in my dad's knees when he bent to clean a sink, the heat rising off the highway that afternoon.

Because that's where leadership starts, not in corner offices, but in the quiet spaces where character is tested.

You Can Grow Without Selling Out

Some people hit a little success and immediately start acting like the world owes them a parade. They buy the shiny car, change their tone, forget who helped them, and start talking down to the very people who keep their life running.

But the ones who move through life with real strength—the ones who rise and *stay* risen—are the ones who stay grounded. They don't forget the early mornings, the dirty jobs, the people who showed up for them when nobody else would.

They don't forget the rag they used to wipe the sink, or the hands that rolled up the tarps. They carry that same blue-collar spirit into every room they enter.

Handle what's in front of you. Leave things better than you found them. Respect the people who make your world possible. That's what my dad would've done. It's what I've always tried to do.

Because growing doesn't mean forgetting. You can climb higher without losing your roots. You can earn more without pretending it makes you more.

Success Is Not a Personality Replacement Plan

Climbing the ladder doesn't require changing who you are. It requires remembering who built the ladder for you.

It's easy to think success demands reinvention—that you have to talk different, act different, network different. But the truth is, the world's full of people trying to look important. The ones who are important are the ones who remember how to treat people.

Real success amplifies your origin story. It gives you the stage and the microphone—so you can bring others with you.

Because if your success isolates you from the people who remind you where you came from, it's not success. It's a costume.

The Restroom Test

Every time I walk into an airport lounge or executive suite, I think about that day on the road.

The heat. The smell of diesel. My dad's voice.

I watch as the porters quietly clean up the mess left behind by fellow travelers, and notice when a bathroom attendant takes pride in their job, keeping their work area spotless.

And I silently ask myself: Would he be proud of the man I've become? Would that ten-year-old kid recognize me?

That's my filter. Not the revenue number. Not the bonus check. Just that simple test of decency.

Because if success costs you your humility, it's the most expensive mistake you'll ever make.

You can have the corner office. You can have the title, the comp plan, the view.

Just remember to leave the door unlocked for the next person who's still rolling up tarps in the heat, wondering if they'll ever get to come inside.

STOP AND REFLECT

What do you do today that would make your younger self proud and your father nod in approval? And what "executives only" signs might still exist in your own life like the walls, judgments, or blind spots you've built without realizing it?

Have you ever caught yourself acting like the "executives only" guy, dismissing, overlooking, or underestimating someone? What would it look like to lead with gratitude instead?

That day on the truck stuck with me longer than the diesel smell ever did. It lit a quiet fire I still carry to this day. It taught me two things that shaped the rest of my life:

1. Never forget where you came from.
2. Never let someone else decide your ceiling.

Because standing there, covered in grime, barred from a restroom by a man who thought a title made him royalty, I made a quiet promise to myself:

I was going to build a life where nobody could lock a door on me again. Not with a sign. Not with a title. Not with a paycheck.

I didn't come from money. I didn't have an inheritance or a head start. What I had was a front-row seat to hard work, dignity, and the difference between people who build their life and people who coast through it.

And when I finally got old enough to make my own moves, I realized that wealth isn't something you stumble into—it's something you *design*, brick by brick, decision by decision… starting with the first one that feels a little impossible.

For me, that moment came when I was twenty-three years old, staring at a rent increase that pushed me from *comfortable* into *fed up.*

And that's where the real wealth creation story begins.

CHAPTER 23
HOW I BUILT WEALTH FROM NOTHING (AND HOW YOU CAN DO IT FASTER)

Because ownership, not luck, is where freedom begins.

When I look back at my life, it's wild to realize that every financial advantage I enjoy today started because I refused to pay another hundred dollars in rent.

In 2001, I was twenty-three years old, making about $65,000 a year, and living in an apartment where the landlord announced rent was going up from $700 to $800 a month. It wasn't the rent that bothered me—it was the idea that I was working hard, paying every bill on time, and building absolutely nothing. So, I bought my first home.

I know the landscape of home ownership looks very different today, and I don't want this to feel like one of those back-in-my-day stories. My experience wasn't about luck or timing so much as being willing to go where opportunity actually was.

When I moved to Colorado Springs, it was still a small, overlooked town. Most of my California friends thought I was out of my mind. But the cost of living was cheap, and the housing market made it possible for someone young and hungry to get started.

My first property was a tiny half-duplex, 700 square feet, two bedrooms, one bath. The neighborhood wasn't great—people at work joked that I lived in the ghetto—but I didn't care. It was mine.

My mortgage payment, including insurance and property tax, was $700 a month—less than my rent would have been. I could deduct the interest from my taxes. I didn't know it yet, but that one decision—owning something—was the first real wealth move I ever made.

Success Principle #1: Own Something Early

The single most important financial step you'll ever take is moving from consumer to owner. You can't build equity in something you don't own.

I moved in, patched the walls, planted rose bushes, and spent a few nights sitting in the backyard, looking at what I'd built. Then, because I was twenty-three and full of stupid ideas, I bought a used hot tub.

I figured if I had a hot tub, it would be full of women in bikinis every weekend and I'd be the host with the most. It didn't quite work out that way—but it did teach me my first DIY lesson in voltage, danger, and improvisation.

My buddy Tim and I hauled the thing home on a rental trailer, held down by one chain that looked like it belonged on a bicycle. On the drive back, the tub slid halfway off the trailer, and we had to stop to shove it back into place. When I finally got it home, I realized I couldn't just plug it in—I needed a custom 220-volt line.

I couldn't afford an electrician, so I went to Home Depot, bought the parts, and wired it myself. I knocked out power to my entire house once, but somehow didn't electrocute myself. I got it running eventually. I was clueless, reckless, and figuring things out as I went—but that's kind of been my formula ever since.

Success Principle #2: Action Beats Perfection

You don't need to know everything to start. You just have to start. Every successful person I've met learned most of what they know after taking the leap.

From One Door to Many

A couple of years later, life took a turn. My girlfriend got pregnant—and then we found out it was twins. That's when the 700-square-foot duplex started to feel more like a broom closet.

I found a For Sale by Owner sign in a nicer neighborhood—three bedrooms, two baths, corner lot, fruit trees, and a view of Pikes Peak. I made an offer, he accepted, and I moved in. I rented out my duplex to two college girls who promised they'd take good care of the place.

Six months later, the roses were dead, the lawn was brown, and the hot tub had turned into a swamp. The girls had parties every night and smoked indoors despite what the lease said. When I inspected the place, one of their bedroom doors had been kicked in.

That was my first crash course in land lording. The dream of passive income met the reality of human behavior. I realized I wasn't just a property owner—I was running a business.

Success Principle #3: Systems Protect You from People

Good tenants, like good employees, are rare. Set standards, screen carefully, and document everything. Boundaries make business sustainable.

Despite the horror stories, I kept going. In the early 2000s, if you had decent credit, banks would hand you money like candy. No money down, no questions asked. I bought one property after another, renting them out, chasing the dream of passive income.

By 2008, I had around ten properties. Half my tenants were great. The other half were disasters—late rent, parties, police, damage. I spent nights wondering what the hell I'd gotten myself into. When the Great Financial Crisis hit, I decided to change my playbook.

Instead of rehabbing and re-renting trashed houses, I flipped them. I sold the low-end properties, reinvested the profits, and kept only the ones in good neighborhoods. It was stressful, but it forced me to start thinking like an investor instead of a hobbyist.

There were plenty of times I thought I was about to lose it all, moments that reminded me of my dad, when he tried to scale his little trucking business by adding a second truck and everything nearly fell apart. I kept waiting for that same collapse to come for me. But somehow, it never did. Each risk held; each plan worked just enough to keep me in the game.

Success Principle #4: Know When to Pivot

Holding forever isn't always the answer. Sometimes the smartest move isn't more growth—it's a controlled retreat that sets you up for your next play.

My 401(k) Rollercoaster

While all this was happening, I was working at HP, contributing just enough to my 401(k) to get the full match—6 percent. It grew to about $25,000.

When I went to buy my next home in 2005, I did something I don't recommend: I cashed out the 401(k) to fund the down payment. Looking back, it was one of the most expensive decisions I ever made. Had I left that money alone, compounded over the years, it would be worth several times that amount today.

But it taught me something: No one saves their way to wealth by accident. You have to make it automatic.

After that, I raised my 401(k) contributions to 10 percent. Unfortunately, I made another classic rookie move, and I put 100 percent of it into HP stock. I thought I was being loyal. I was really just being dumb. When HP went through tough times, my retirement savings went nowhere.

When I left HP, I rolled the money into a self-directed IRA and started a new 401(k) at Arrow Electronics. This time, I invested entirely in the S&P 500. No day trading, no hero moves—just slow, steady compounding. I learned that boring beats brilliant most of the time.

Success Principle #5: Be the Tortoise, Not the Trader

"Compound interest is the eighth wonder of the world. He who understands it, earns it; he who doesn't, pays it."—Warren Buffet

Wealth doesn't always come from guessing right; it comes from staying in the game. The market rewards consistency, rarely cleverness.

Dollar-cost averaging (investing small, steady amounts over time) is one of the most powerful wealth-building habits you can develop. It keeps emotion out of the equation and ensures you're always buying, no matter what the market is doing. That's the tortoise approach. It's how real wealth compounds quietly in the background, year after year.

Success Principle #6: Take One Bold Shot per Decade

Occasionally, you'll see an opportunity that scares you because it's big. If your gut and research agree, take it, especially when you're young. One good risk can change your trajectory. And every once in a while, the world hands you a once-in-a-decade moment, a chance to make a bold move while everyone else is frozen.

I've always believed in consistency, but I also believe in conviction.

When I left Arrow, I rolled my 401(k) into a self-directed IRA and made one of my best long-term bets: I bought Facebook stock on IPO day. It was chaos; systems crashed, prices swung wildly, and most investors called it a disaster. But I believed in what they were building, that it would change the world, so I held tight. That single decision became a cornerstone win in my portfolio.

Then came 2020.

I remember sitting by the pool in Cabo San Lucas when COVID hit and the market went into free fall. Every day it was down so hard that trading had to be halted. The experts all said the same thing: *"There's nothing you can do. Just ride it out."*

But my gut and years of watching opportunity hide inside panic told me otherwise.

I sold a portion of our portfolio, waited a couple of weeks, and started buying Amazon stock at prices that made no sense for a company that dominant, which would soon become a lifeline for folks trapped at home. It was a calculated bet, not a gamble, grounded in belief, timing, and data.

The rest is history. It became one of the most significant wins of my investing career.

If I could give you one piece of advice with regard to investing, this would be it. Keep investing steadily, but when the world loses its mind, and you *know* what you believe in, that's when you earn the right to take a swing.

Success Principle #7: Build Wealth as a Team

If you're married or in a partnership, your financial future is a shared mission. Two people saving together move twice as fast and argue half as much.

As the years went by, our real estate appreciated, and our investments compounded. We had incorporated years earlier and treated our rentals like a business. That structure gave us tax advantages—write-offs for computers, phones, even the occasional meal when we discussed how to expand our business.

People think real estate is passive income. It's not. It's a time-consuming business. It's a tough business. But if you manage it right, it becomes a financial engine that runs quietly in the background, paying down your properties and throwing off cash flow while you sleep.

Rewarding the Climb

I'd love to say we were stoic minimalists who never rewarded ourselves, but that would be a lie. When we hit a $1 million net worth, we opened a bottle of Caymus. When we hit $2 million, I bought a Rolex. When we crossed $3 million, my wife got her Louboutin bag.

I wrote earlier in this book that you should celebrate the little things—and that includes the milestones. Just don't mistake them for the finish line.

We've never inherited much, but any time we did, or came into a little windfall, we used it wisely—paying off credit cards, funding our kids' college accounts, or adding to our investments. Windfalls are like lightning strikes: bright, unpredictable, and fleeting. If you don't direct that energy, it'll burn you instead of fueling you.

Success Principle #8: Create Extra Lanes of Income

Never depend on one paycheck. Build side hustles, passive income, and investment streams that protect you when one lane slows down.

The eBay Hustle

When HP started showing cracks, I launched that side business I told you about earlier out of my garage selling returned merchandise on eBay. I discovered a local mail-order company was dumping its returns, of cheap Chinese made items, at a thrift store for tax write-offs.

I bought their stuff for $1–3 and resold it online for $20–50. Soon I was making over $10,000 a month, netting half that in profit. I used that money to pay down mortgages and invest in stocks.

Eventually, competitors flooded the market, the mail-order company folded, and the margins vanished. I even tried importing directly from China, but it became a race to the bottom.

That's when I learned one of the most important lessons in business: Never compete on price.

Compete on value.

Compete on service.

Compete on experience.

Because when you compete on price, you've already lost.

Running the Numbers

For nearly twenty years, my wife and I have tracked every aspect of our finances in spreadsheets—income, spending, investments, credit cards, even monthly subscriptions. We look at them like a pilot checks instruments.

Each tab tells a story: where the money went, how the market performed, what went up or down, and why. This habit has kept us aligned, honest, and focused. It's also given us the confidence to make big decisions—because we can see, in black and white, where we stand.

Success Principle #9: Measure Everything That Matters

If you can't measure it, you can't improve it. Run your finances like a business—with dashboards, trends, and accountability.

The Power of a Planner

When we turned forty-five, we hired a Certified Financial Planner named Mark. He reviewed everything I'd built—the investments, real estate, retirement accounts—and said the words every planner dreams of saying: "You're on track."

We should have done it years earlier. A good financial planner doesn't just optimize your money—they referee your marriage. Mark helped us align goals, understand risk tolerance, and make smart trade-offs. He also confirmed that we could soon hit our next big milestone: a second home in Scottsdale.

You need someone who knows how to zoom out when you're too close to the details. Someone to remind you that the plan isn't just about money—it's about freedom.

Success Principle #10: Build a Plan That Outlives You

Wealth without structure evaporates. Plan for your family, your future, and your legacy—because money that isn't managed will manage you.

My Financial Success Blueprint

For those who like checklists, here's the condensed version of how I did it—and how you can do it faster:

1. Buy early. Even a small starter home teaches you more about money than any class ever will.
2. Treat real estate like a business. Systems, leases, rules—run it tight.
3. Automate investing. The S&P 500 and compound interest will do the heavy lifting.
4. Max out your 401(k)s. Especially if you're married—double the contributions, halve the taxes.
5. Use ESPPs (employee stock purchase plans) and RSUs as accelerators. But diversify once they vest.
6. Track your numbers monthly. Know your inflows, outflows, and net worth.
7. Hire a planner early. They'll see blind spots before you do.
8. Take one big bet every decade but be sure of yourself when you do.

9. Celebrate milestones. They're markers on a long road, not finish lines.
10. Create multiple income streams. Security comes from options, not luck.
11. Play the long game. Time and discipline beat timing and genius every single time.

When I bought that half-duplex in 2001, I had no overarching plan. I just wanted to stop wasting rent money. But that one decision set off a chain reaction that changed everything.

Wealth doesn't come from brilliance—it comes from intention, from putting your money to work instead of letting it sit still. If you can live below your means, invest consistently, and treat your finances like a business, you will win. Maybe not overnight, but inevitably.

And if you do it right, you'll get to the point where you can finally look out over the mountain, glass of Caymus in hand, and realize:

It wasn't luck. It was discipline. It was time. And it was worth every minute of the climb.

STOP AND REFLECT

What's one thing you could own—not rent, borrow, or subscribe to—that would start building equity in your life today? (Your answer might not be real estate; it could be a business, a brand, or even a skill.)

What would your one bold bet per decade look like—the move that scares you, but could change everything if you're right? Do you have the conviction, research, and risk plan to take that swing when the moment comes?

If you share your financial life with someone, are you operating like a team or like two individuals? When's the last time you held a real "financial meeting" together with goals, metrics, and next steps?

Building wealth from nothing taught me a lot about money. But raising two daughters taught me everything about *value*. Because here's the truth most people never figure out:

Money is math.

Wealth is discipline.

But legacy? That's altogether something different.

I used real estate, risk, side hustles, and long-game investing to build a financial foundation brick by brick—but the whole time, in the background, I was building something even more important: two future adults who would one day have to navigate this world without me there to catch them.

All the spreadsheets, the properties, the wins, the losses—they were never the point. They were just the tools I used to become the kind of man my kids could learn from. Because it doesn't matter how high you climb if the next generation can't build on the ground you broke for them.

So, after years of figuring out how to build wealth the hard way, I realized something even more critical. If you don't teach your kids how to think, how to work, how to compete, and how to carry themselves... they'll spend their adulthood cleaning up problems you could've prevented in childhood.

And that's why the next chapter matters more than anything I've written so far. This isn't about money. It's about the people who will inherit the world you're building—and whether they'll be ready for it.

Let's talk about raising winners in a world that rewards softness.

CHAPTER 24
RAISING WINNERS: BUILDING STRONG, INDEPENDENT KIDS IN A SOFT WORLD

Because our job isn't to protect them from the world, it's to prepare them for it.

People sometimes tell me, "Your daughters take after you."

It's the greatest compliment I could ever receive. It almost brings me to tears, every time.

I can't take full credit for how they turned out since I only had shared custody while they were growing up, but I tried to fit as much life, love, and learning into the time we had together as humanly possible.

And somehow, through all the chaos, it worked.

Whatever your situation, every parent shares a common mission: to raise resilient, capable, and grounded kids. Children who can thrive in a cold, competitive world, who can pay their own bills, build real skills, push through hard times, and still find joy along the way. Kids who grow into happy, healthy adults that choose their mates wisely, because nothing shapes your life more than who you build it with.

We've all seen the opposite: the adult basement dwellers, the ones who chased useless degrees, dropped out or got stuck in relationships that hollowed them out. The thirty-somethings whose parents are still covering their insurance and phone bills because somewhere along the line, the hard lessons never came.

This chapter is here to help you avoid that and to raise kids who don't just survive the real world, but dominate it. Kids who know how to think, earn, love, and live with purpose.

Success Principle #1: Time Is the Real Currency

When it comes to raising kids, quality time beats quantity every time. You don't need every day, you just need to make the days you get count.

Some parents put a baseball in their kid's crib. Others, a doll. I read mine stories about great business leaders and turned CNBC into background music in the house.

From the moment they were old enough to notice, I'd point to the screen and ask, "Is the market up or down today?"

They learned that green meant up and red meant down before they could tie their shoes.

As they grew, when we walked into any business together, it could be a restaurant, it could be a store, I would turn to them and say, "Explain to me how you think this place makes money?"

They got into a habit of analyzing businesses and seeing the flow of the dollar throughout the operation in front of them, from the time they were five years old. Deal size, volume, margins, all became regular dinner table conversation.

I wanted them to walk through life, not just as consumers, but as future business owners.

Turning Life into a Game

As I mentioned earlier, competition was something I encouraged from day one. I'd read a story once about how Bill Gates's grandmother turned everything in her house into a competition, and I thought, *That's genius*.

So, I did the same.

Who could clean up the fastest? Who could say their ABCs first? Who could bring me the most blocks? Who could eat their lunch first? Who could stay off the teacher's bad list the longest?

I was raising two little gladiators in a world full of participation trophies, and I wanted them to understand that real life doesn't hand out ribbons just for showing up.

Success Principle #2: Make Winning Normal

You should never apologize for raising competitive kids. The world rewards effort, discipline, and follow-through, not feelings.

Monopoly Lessons

Once they could count, we started playing Monopoly.

They loved it: hiding money, building strategy, making deals.

Scarlet became famous for collecting all the railroads. She'd negotiate until you couldn't take it anymore and finally caved. Avery loved watching people land on her hotels, counting out every last bill as if she was shaking them upside down for loose change.

They didn't realize it, but they were learning negotiation, asset management, and delayed gratification; skills most adults still struggle with.

The Lemonade Stand Hustle

When the weekend rolled around, and they'd say, "Dad, we're bored," my response was automatic: "Then start a business."

They'd set up lemonade stands in the front yard, waving down cars and figuring out which corner signs pulled the most traffic. They learned marketing, sales, and the value of effort, one cup at a time.

On other weekends, we'd cruise garage sales. That's where they learned to negotiate in the real world. I'd model the process—make an offer, counter, smile, walk away—and they picked it up instantly.

Soon, they never paid full price for anything again. People would melt when a five-year-old asked, "Will you take a dollar?"

Sometimes they got the item for free. That's what happens when you learn the power of charm early.

Success Principle #3: Teach Hustle Early

Work ethic isn't inherited, it's modeled. If kids see you negotiate, they'll negotiate. If they see you grind, they'll grind.

Jobs, Chores, and the $1 Bag of Pinecones

In our house, work was expected—not as punishment, but to make money. Clean the baseboards. Wash the windows. Pick up pinecones. These were all paid jobs.

I'd hand them plastic grocery bags and say, "You get $1 for every full bag of pinecones you bring me."

Once Scarlet took my lessons on sales and entrepreneurship a little too far when she wanted $10 for something at school in second grade. I told her, "Figure out how to earn it."

She grabbed some crayons, drew an elephant, walked to the street, flagged down a car, and closed the guy, on the spot, for $10.

To this day, we have no idea who that buyer was, but I've never been prouder. She tells that story in job interviews now.

Another time when the kids wanted to make cash, I showed them how to build simple wooden planter boxes from old scraps in our garage that they could sell out on the driveway to passersby. This was a valuable lesson in both product manufacturing and sales. They quickly saw how a handful of screws and some old planks could be turned into profit.

After sales were slow from drive-by traffic, they quickly decided to take these planters door to door in order to drum up sales. While I was expecting them to sell the planters for $5 or $10, they came home that afternoon after selling out at $40 per unit. I shook my head, laughing, in disbelief.

Good News / Bad News

At dinner, we had a nightly ritual called Good News / Bad News.

Each of us shared one thing that went well that day and one thing that didn't.

We didn't just talk about what went wrong—we problem-solved together.

It was our way of building emotional intelligence, communication, and accountability, the same values that drive great teams in business.

Success Principle #4: Debrief the Day

Teach your kids to reflect. The ability to analyze wins and losses daily builds maturity faster than any class ever could.

Cheer, Grit, and Follow-Through

Both girls got into cheerleading in high school. They'd come home sore and frustrated, saying they wanted to quit. I'd tell them, "Okay, you can quit tomorrow."

But by morning, they'd get up, put on their uniform, and go again. That's grit: the ability to keep going when comfort whispers "stop."

Later in college, they joined sororities, where they learned the politics, teamwork, and leadership that would shape their adult lives. They still wanted to quit sometimes but never did.

Success Principle #5: Let Them Quit Tomorrow

Never force a child to love something. But don't let them quit in the heat of frustration either. Endurance is learned one "I'll try again tomorrow" at a time.

Choosing the Right Major

When it came time for college, we made a controversial move: We picked their majors.

We talked through their interests, their strengths, sure, but as the investors footing most of the bill, we wanted a say in how the capital was deployed.

I think it's also important to note that letting an eighteen-year-old make a decision like that alone, that can impact them for the rest of their lives, is putting a lot on someone, especially someone who really lacks the capacity to make such a hefty call.

For parents out there who think that little Johnny should be allowed to choose whatever he wants to study in school, and he should be fully funded to do so, please consider how irresponsible and dangerous this might be for your child's future.

I told them, "We're not paying for a four-year vacation. We're paying for you to build a foundation for independence."

They understood. They agreed that business and communications would be the best choices—degrees that would actually pay the bills. Versatile degrees that they could use to go in any direction they wanted, as they developed into grown adults.

Now that both have graduated, they're each working as Sales Development Reps (SDRs), getting punched in the mouth by rejection every day, and thriving, as they make cold calls. It doesn't faze them, because they were raised to expect life to hit back.

Success Principle #6: Prepare Them for the Punches

Don't raise kids to avoid rejection, raise them to recover from it. Confidence comes from surviving failure, not escaping it.

Parenting with Help

The journey wasn't always easy. Working full time and with shared custody, meant there were times I felt like I was trying to teach life lessons through a keyhole, squeezing everything important into weekends and holidays.

During the year I commuted to my job in Denver, I felt immense guilt when I would drop the girls off every morning at 7 a.m. and be the last to pick them up at 6 p.m., from childcare, on my way home. We barely had time to sit down for dinner, before it was time to get ready for bed, but we squeezed as much as we could into those brief windows.

Of course, like all parents, there were rough patches, disagreements, tears, and learning curves.

That's why my wife and I sought professional advice over the years through child psychologists and family therapists, not because we were failing, but because we knew we didn't have all the answers.

Getting advice from experts, when we needed it, proved to be invaluable, and would be something I would highly recommend to all parents out there trying to go it alone.

A good therapist is like a great CSM: they don't live your life for you, they just show you the path to value.

Success Principle #7: Ask for Backup

Even great parents need coaching. Don't wait until the wheels come off to get help. Strong families ask questions early.

The Result

Now my daughters are grown; they are independent, resilient, and armed with the confidence to carve out their own lives. They understand money, they know how to work, they know how to compete, and they've learned that comfort never built anything worth having.

Every time someone tells me, "Your daughters remind me of you," I smile not because I see myself in them, but because I see the best parts of who I always hoped to be.

Success Principle #8: Model the Life You Want Them to Build

Kids don't become who you tell them to be; they become who you are when you think they're not watching.

If I had to sum up my parenting philosophy in one line, it would be this:

"Raise them like the world's not going to cut them any slack because it won't."

I didn't raise them to need me. I raised them to know they'd be okay when I wasn't there.

And that, to me, is the ultimate definition of success.

A few weeks ago, my daughter Avery called me in tears. She's been working as an SDR grinding, learning, and competing every day in one of the toughest jobs there is. She'd won Sales Rep of the Month twice in a row, and that third month, she came in second missing it by only 1 client demo.

She was devastated.

She'd worked her ass off. She'd gotten used to the recognition, the number one spot, the feeling of winning, and when she didn't get it this time, it crushed her.

I listened. I let her vent. Then I said,

"Avery, if you're this upset about coming in second place, then I must have done a damn good job raising you, because I don't think there are a lot of kids out there like you anymore."

She laughed through the tears. And I could feel that mix of pride and pain only a parent understands: the moment you realize your kid has inherited your fire, and it burns just as bright.

STOP AND REFLECT

Are you setting the bar high enough for your kids—or are you lowering it so they'll like you? What's one standard, rule, or expectation you've let slide lately that's costing them resilience?

What do the young people in your life actually *see* when they watch you?

Would you be proud if they copied your habits, your work ethic, and your response to adversity?

Are you protecting your kids from failure or preparing them to face it?

How can you give them just enough struggle to build strength without breaking their spirit?

Would the young people in your life survive and thrive in a world without participation trophies? What can you do *this week* to start toughening their mindset with love and purpose?

Raising winners is one thing. Raising *the next generation of leaders* is another.

And after my daughters grew into strong, sharp, independent women—after I watched them build their own lives with the same grit I tried to instill in them—I realized something bigger:

Parenting is only the first half of the job. The second half is what you leave behind when the job is done. Because eventually, your kids won't need you to tie their shoes, check their homework, or walk them through their first heartbreak.

What they *will* need—long after you're gone—is a roadmap. Not just money. Not just memories. But a system. A foundation. A philosophy they can inherit.

Raising winners is about today. Legacy is about tomorrow—and every tomorrow after that.

At some point, we all face the same quiet question in the middle of the night:

"If I disappeared tomorrow... would my family still rise, or would everything I built disappear with me?"

If raising my daughters taught me anything, it's that strength alone isn't enough. You have to leave something behind that keeps them strong when you can't.

That's where we go next.

Let's talk about legacy—and how to build something that outlives you.

CHAPTER 25
LEGACY PLANNING: BUILD SOMETHING THAT OUTLIVES YOU

You don't need to have kids to want to leave something behind on this Earth, when you are gone. Maybe it's an idea that will outlive you, or a lasting change that you made while you were here. Maybe it's a foundation, maybe it's a statue. Maybe it's a dent in the universe.

In my case, leaving a legacy means that when I'm gone, my family will be taken care of financially, and have fond memories of the impact I made on their lives. I hope to positively impact the lives of my grandchildren, who aren't yet born, and their children too. I hope they look back and remember me as the one who changed everything. "The One."

When my parents died, they didn't leave much of a financial legacy. My half brother and half sister and I were grateful to come away with a little money, after we sold their house, but to me it felt heartbreakingly small for two lives lived so long, for two people who loved their family and dreamed of providing for future generations.

It wasn't for lack of work or heart. It was for lack of a plan. They never discussed money in detail. The only time they invested in the stock market was the year leading up to the dot-com bust. Burned badly, they stuck with savings accounts after.

They never bought or held real estate beyond their home, except an early foray into the Austin rental market in 1978 that produced almost no profit and a lot of headaches thanks to the oil crisis.

Some might say they had extraordinarily bad luck; however, those who understand compound interest would say that their real misfortune was never learning how time quietly rewards even the smallest, most consistent investments.

If they had simply taken a little money they earned throughout their lives and parked it in the S&P 500, it would have compounded into many millions by the time they passed. Instead, it was gone, quietly spent, eroded by time, taxes, slot machines, and life's curveballs.

That reality shook me. Because my parents weren't careless; they were just unprepared.

And I decided right then that the story would end differently with me.

At some point, every person who's ever built anything that mattered has the same quiet thought:

What happens if I'm not here tomorrow?

You don't say it out loud. You just feel it. Late at night, when the house is quiet and everyone you love is asleep, you stare at the ceiling and wonder:

Would they be okay? Would they know what to do? Would the systems I built still protect them when I can't?

That's not fear. That's leadership.

Because true success isn't about what happens while you're here. It's about what happens after.

The Systems You Build Should Outlive You

If there's one thing enterprise software and fatherhood have in common, it's this:

Systems are what protect you when chaos hits.

I am reminded of a night when our twins, at five years old, both erupted into a violent night of vomiting in bed that lasted until 3 a.m. I was grateful we had stocked all those extra towels, sheets, and blankets, just in case.

A family, like a business, needs infrastructure—routines, clarity, access, and accountability.

If your systems are strong, your spouse will have confidence instead of confusion. Your kids will have guidance instead of grief. And your name will carry weight, not because you were perfect, but because you planned for their peace.

It's not about money. It's about resilience by design.

Every Family Has "The One"

Look through any family tree long enough and you'll see it.

Generations of good people living quietly—working hard, paying bills, doing their best—until one name stands out.

The One.

The one who changed the trajectory. The one who decided mediocrity wasn't an inheritance worth passing down. The one who broke the pattern, rewrote the script, and built something that would last.

Every great family in history has one: the Rockefellers, the Carnegies, the Johnsons.

But there are millions of smaller, untold stories too of families who quietly transformed their entire lineage because one person said, "It stops with me."

So ask yourself:

Will I be "The One" for my family?

The Questions That Keep Me Honest

If I were gone tomorrow, would my family know what to do? Would my systems hold? Would they still have clarity, income, and guidance, or would they be lost in the fog, trying to guess my passwords and piece together my intentions?

And beyond that: Would anyone remember me in a year? Ten years? A hundred years?

Would my name be spoken around dinner tables by people who never met me—because the decisions I made still shape the life they're living?

Or would I fade quietly into family history, another generation that "did fine"?

Legacy is measured by how long your impact echoes.

The Difference Between Wealth and Legacy

Wealth is numbers. Legacy is meaning.

Wealth can vanish. Legacy compounds.

You can leave behind cash, stocks, and property, but if you don't leave behind wisdom, systems, traditions, and values, the fortune disappears by the second or third generation.

They call it shirtsleeves to shirtsleeves because families that gain wealth without guidance lose it again within three generations.

That's not destiny. That's poor design. And you can design something better.

Build a Family Operating System

If you can run a $50M business, you can run your family the same way—with intention, communication, and a playbook.

1. Document Everything.
   Accounts, passwords, insurance, legal contacts because these are the map that keeps them from guessing.
2. Explain the "Why."
   Don't just leave instructions. Leave understanding. Why you invested, why you saved, why you built what you did.
3. Train for Stewardship.
   Teach your kids to manage money, responsibility, and relationships before you hand them the keys.
4. Appoint Your Board.
   Every family needs trusted advisers: financial, legal, emotional. Build your bench now, not after you're gone.
5. Pass Down Rituals, Not Just Assets.
   Legacy isn't just in wills and trusts; it's in family dinners, annual trips, and the stories that shape identity.

The "If I'm Gone" Plan

This isn't morbid. It's love in its most practical form.

If you were gone tomorrow, could your spouse open one folder, physical or digital, and know exactly what to do? Who to call? How to access accounts? Where the insurance documents are? How to keep things running?

That's not paranoia; that's preparedness. And it's one of the most selfless gifts you can leave behind.

Because when the worst happens, clarity becomes currency.

Designing for One-Hundred Years

It's easy to think short-term, e.g., to plan for college, for retirement, for when the kids are grown.

But legacy demands you think in centuries.

If your systems are strong, your name won't vanish in a decade. It'll live in the habits, confidence, and freedom of the people who carry it forward.

Imagine your great-grandchildren talking about you, not as a ghost, but as the one who changed it all. The one who built the foundation they're standing on. The one who left behind more than money, who left behind a philosophy.

That's the kind of immortality worth working for.

From Fragile to Forever

Every family has a turning point. The moment when struggle becomes structure. When surviving becomes thriving. That turning point can be you.

If you build the systems now, if you document, teach, and protect, you give your family more than comfort. You give them continuity.

You become the hinge that swings your entire family line from fragile to forever.

If you were gone tomorrow, what would remain of you a year from now?

Ten years? A hundred?

Would your family still be standing strong because of what you built or standing still because you never did?

Would they tell stories about how you changed it all or would your name fade into quiet footnotes?

The answer to that question isn't fate. It's design.

So, build systems that last. Protect what matters. Be the one who ends the excuses and begins the legacy.

Because someday, someone will trace your family line back to you, and they'll say, "That's where it started."

STOP AND REFLECT

If you were gone tomorrow, could your family open one folder and know exactly what to do?

Or would they be left guessing your passwords, plans, and priorities?

Every family has The One, the person who changes everything.

Are you building systems, habits, and traditions that make you that person?

What decision could you make *this year* that your great-grandchildren would still benefit from?

Think beyond money: What belief, value, or ritual deserves to outlive you?

Legacy isn't built in a boardroom or inside a spreadsheet. It's built in the little moments nobody else sees.

It's built in the nights you stay up organizing documents so your family never has to guess. It's built in the routines, the rituals, the systems that keep the people you love safe long after you're gone. It's built in the decisions you make today that echo into a future you'll never get to see.

But here's the part most people miss:

Legacy isn't only about the future.

It's also about honoring the journey that brought you here.

Because before you can look forward with clarity, you have to be brave enough to look back with gratitude. Back at the beginning. Back at the people who shaped you. Back at the moments that felt ordinary at the time but ended up defining everything.

And sometimes, the deepest lessons aren't found in the inheritance you leave behind, they're found in the memories you carry with you. For me, that realization didn't hit in a financial planner's office or while building a trust.

It hit in the most unexpected place:

On an old zoo path I used to walk as a broke single dad, pulling a red wagon full of sticky-fingered toddlers and peanut-butter sandwiches… and then decades later walking the same path in a tuxedo, surrounded by other wealthy donors.

Sometimes the only way to understand the mountain you've climbed is to revisit the place where the climb began.

Let's go there.

CHAPTER 26
THE VIEW FROM THE MOUNTAIN

Because gratitude isn't found at the summit, it's built along the way.

The Broke Dad at the Zoo

When my daughters were little, the zoo was everything.

I was a broke single dad then, holding on by my fingernails. Every dollar mattered; every decision carried weight. But no matter how tight the budget was, I made sure we had a zoo pass.

It wasn't luxury, it was escape. It was a few hours where life didn't feel like survival.

I'd pack peanut-butter and jelly sandwiches and juice, stuff diapers and wipes into a backpack, and load the twins into their big red double wagon. I'd spend whole Saturdays and sometimes Sundays too, pulling them up the hills of the Cheyenne Mountain Zoo, going from the lions to elephants to monkeys, their sticky fingers clutching sippy cups, their laughter echoing behind me.

We never got bored, because we could always use our imaginations, or come up with something fun to do, whether we were pretending to be crossing the Serengeti on safari or going to visit the Queen once we reached the top of the mountain. Spoiler alert: She always seemed to be on vacation when we got there.

We went every single weekend for years, rain, snow, or shine. It was our ritual, and something we looked forward to throughout the week. We'd keep track of which animals were having babies that we could go visit, or when the zoo would transform into a winter wonderland to welcome Santa Claus each December.

Sometimes we stayed until the park closed, because walking those shaded paths felt better than going home to a dark house with bills stacked on the counter. The girls would often fall asleep on the drive home, and I'd be ready for bed myself, but still needed to cook dinner and give baths.

When the girls were four, Erin joined our family and helped introduce them to so many firsts in that zoo: their first carousel ride, first train ride, and first pony ride. Taking them for the annual Boo at the Zoo event was always a fun time, because the zoo transformed into a spooky, haunted place at night, where the kids could trick or treat, and we'd get to observe what the animals do after dark.

Looking back, it's funny how perspective changes everything. At the time, I thought those years were some of the hardest of my life—scraping by, exhausted, trying to figure out how to be a good dad while keeping the lights on. But now, I see them for what they really were: Some of the best memories I'll ever have.

We didn't have much, but inside those zoo gates, we had everything that mattered: laughter, imagination, curiosity, and the kind of love that grows stronger each day.

It's amazing how time redefines struggle.

The Same Paths, Years Later

Fast-forward many years.

Erin and I were walking those same paths again last year, but this time we were dressed in black-tie, surrounded by chandeliers and string lights at the Zoo Ball.

It was almost surreal. The same place where I once pushed a stroller was now filled with tuxedos and gowns, champagne flutes clinking, and a jazz trio playing near the giraffe exhibit.

I looked around that ballroom and felt the collision of two worlds: the past and the present.

There I was, a kid who'd once counted change at the gas pump, standing among people who'd clearly been born into comfort with names on buildings, old money, trust funds, lives that started miles ahead of mine.

And yet, in that moment, I felt something powerful: I belonged here.

Not because of what was in my bank account, but because of what it took to get here.

What Money Couldn't Teach Me

My dad retired from the Air Force with a chest full of medals, two ex-wives and PTSD. What I always admired most was that my dad was never bitter about it. He could have been; he had every reason to be, but that just wasn't who he was. He took life as it came, with a shrug, a joke, and a stubborn pride that came from understanding that he wasn't entitled to anything in the world.

My mom—British, sarcastic, orderly—kept us moving forward. She'd polish her silver tea set, just in case the Queen decided to stop by for tea and would iron every piece of laundry done in our house right down to my underwear.

They never had wealth, but they had pride, manners, and grit, and those lessons became the backbone of my entire life.

So, standing there at the Zoo Ball, surrounded by people who'd *inherited* their seats at the table, I realized something:

I wouldn't trade what I learned growing up poor for anything these folks were born with.

Growing up broke taught me empathy, adaptability, and the ability to read a room. It taught me to talk to anyone—janitor or CEO—and mean it. It taught me that respect can't be bought, and humility can't be faked.

Those lessons built the man who now stood there in a tux, holding a glass of champagne, quietly thanking the two people who never got to see this view but made it possible.

The View from the Mountain

This fall, I sat by the pool at my country club in Colorado Springs, working on this book on my MacBook, while simultaneously watching football on my iPad, with the vast view of Garden of the Gods and Pikes Peak spread out in front of me.

The air was crisp, the mountains glowing in the afternoon sun, and I thought about that night at the zoo and how far the road had stretched from peanut-butter sandwiches to gala dinners, from fear to peace.

I thought about my parents, my wife, my daughters, and the strange path that had carried us all here.

For most of my life, I thought success was a destination—a title, a salary, a number in the bank.

But sitting there that day, I realized it's not about the finish line. It's about the climb and the gratitude you collect along the way.

The zoo taught me that. The broke years taught me that. Every setback, every win, every bottle opened in celebration: They were all part of the same mountain.

And now, from the top, the view wasn't pride. It was peace.

Success Planning Takeaways

- Your beginnings matter. They're not something to outgrow; they're your foundation.

- Gratitude fuels endurance. Remember where you started; it keeps the climb honest.
- Celebrate progress, not perfection. The small wins are what make the summit meaningful.
  - Write goals on special bottles of wine you'll open when you meet them.
  - Plan little celebrations for when you cross key milestones along the way, like dinners out, or takeout and champagne toasts at home.
- Character outlasts circumstance. What you learn in the lean years becomes your greatest wealth.
- Keep looking back. The view's only beautiful if you remember what it took to get there.

STOP AND REFLECT

Have you been so focused on the summit that you've forgotten to celebrate the steps?

What's one milestone, big or small, you should stop and toast right now?

If you're broke right now, you're not behind; you're just at base-camp.

Every empire, every comeback, every inspirational story starts where you are: with grit, not glory. What's one small step you can take *this week* to start your climb?

What's *your* version of the mountain? Name one goal so big it scares you.

Standing on top of the mountain gives you perspective. It lets you see the whole road: the zoo days, the broke years, the long climbs, the quiet victories nobody ever applauded. It lets you feel grateful for every step, every scar, every stretch of the journey that shaped you.

But the truth people don't like to talk about? The view from the top doesn't erase the price you paid to get there. Success doesn't come with a refund policy. Every mile, every sacrifice, every night you spent grinding instead of sleeping; the bill always shows up eventually.

Gratitude mattered. Reflection mattered. But so did the cost.

Because you don't build a career like mine or any big life without leaving pieces of yourself scattered across airports, hotel rooms, rental cars, and dimly lit steakhouses at 11:45 p.m. You don't win at a high level without paying for it in ways that never make it onto LinkedIn.

That's the part nobody warns you about. The part that hides behind the polished titles, the first-class upgrades, the big numbers, and the smiling photos at customer dinners.

And after all these years, after all the nights staring at ceilings in strange cities, I realized something:

You can admire the mountain...*and still be honest about the toll of the climb.*

That's where we go next.

Let's talk about the real cost of winning and how to keep paying it without going broke.

CHAPTER 27
THE COST OF WINNING

Because every tab comes due—and the house always collects.

Legacy sounds noble on a slide. Winning looks glamorous in a photo. But there's a tab no one posts.

Whether you're an entrepreneur, a salesman, or a CSM like me, there is a hidden cost to winning that all of us will eventually have to pay.

Here's the real price list: the sleepless, staring-at-the-ceiling nights in unfamiliar rooms; the knot between your shoulder blades from nine hours in an airplane seat designed by a sadist; the indigestion from a "great spot" where the food is average but the client loves it—so you smile and love it too. And the miles you put on your liver nursing Old Fashioneds until the customer is ready to go home… then closing the Marriott bar because you're too wired to sleep after the rush.

I have lived that receipt.

There's a moment at every steakhouse where the room tilts from business to bonding—when the second round lands and the conversation loosens. This is the arena. You're reading the table, sensing the currents, deciding when to press and when to shut up. If you do it right, you feel the deal lock into place like a seatbelt. The adrenaline hits. Your body is buzzing and every story lands. For a few hours, you are exactly who you trained to be.

And then the lights go up. The plates are cleared. You tip big because that's who you are. You walk the client to the door, shake hands like you mean it, and the city air hits your face like a reset. Back at the hotel, you don't head to bed—you drift to the lobby bar because you know the truth: You're not coming down yet.

Winning has a hangover that isn't just physical. It's spiritual.

Because after the high, you face the quiet: a dark room, an unreliable HVAC, your mind replaying the night—what you said, where the pivot happened, which promise you just made your future self keep. You stare at the ceiling and barter with sleep. Tomorrow will ask you to do it again. And again. And again.

This is the cost-of-winning treadmill no one warns you about.

The body keeps the score: the stiff back from window at 8A, the tight chest from one too many airport coffees, the reflux from laughing through a ribeye you didn't want, and the "just one more" that turns into three because the table needed it.

The soul keeps the score, too.

If you're not careful, the road becomes your personality, and the rush becomes your religion. You tell yourself it's all for the team, for the number, for the legacy—but the truth is simpler and more dangerous: You love the show. You love the steakhouse arena, the candles, the noise, the closing line that lands so clean you can hear it. You love being needed. And that love can quietly bankrupt the rest of your life.

Here's the line no one puts in their playbook: Your spouse is your #1 customer.

Not metaphorically. Literally.

If the home fires go out, you'll win a lot of dinners and lose the only table that matters. If there's nothing warm to come back to when the lights go down, all the applause is just echo. A deal that closes with no one to call on the walk back to the hotel is a hollow victory. The story you want to tell your grandkids is not "I was the last one at the bar again."

So, we plan the cost of winning, the same way we plan the pursuit of it.

How I pay the price without going broke:

- Pre-commitments at home. Before the trip, I book the date night, schedule the call times, and set the expectation for when I'll be fully offline. I don't "fit family in." I protect it like my biggest account—because it is.
- Ritualized comedown. After the steakhouse, I don't wander. If the hotel is close enough, I walk it. Fifteen minutes outside, a liter of water, hot shower, magnesium, journal three lines: What mattered? What did I promise? What can wait? It's not romantic; it's survival.
- Body tax accounting. One workout every trip, even if it's just twenty minutes. Stretch on the plane. Food rules: protein first, vegetables second, "client favorites" in small bites. I know there is no drink max, but I try to balance with equal parts water and humility.
- Boundaries with grace. I'll stay for the relationship, and for the extra round, when needed. But, if the moment has already landed, I choose the long game and leave on a high note. The next day's follow-through matters more than last night's third hour.
- Honest debriefs at home. When I land, I report like I would to an executive sponsor—wins, worries, and what I owe. I ask the only metric that matters: "Do you still feel like you come first?" If the answer wobbles, I change something now—not after the quarter.

Winning should feel like fuel, not fire. The moment it starts burning your foundation, that's your signal. Not to quit—winners don't quit—but to re-architect the way you win so it doesn't cost the only things that make winning worth it.

The check always comes. Pay it with intention.

Success Plan Notes (pin this to your travel day)

- Home-Fire KPI: Before you fly, text your spouse/partner: "Here are my call windows. What do you need from me this week?" Put it on your calendar.
- Bar-to-Bed Protocol: Walk fifteen minutes outside → water → hot shower → three-line journal → lights out. No hotel-bar heroics.
- Body Nonnegotiables: One workout per trip; stretch before/after flights; eat protein/veg first; cap drinks when you can, until you can't—then match with water.
- Relationship Rule: If staying later only feeds your ego, leave. If it feeds the relationship, stay—then follow through the next day.
- Debrief Script (Home): "Win(s) / Promise(s) I made / What I'm fixing this week. Do you still feel like #1?" Listen to the answer. Adjust.

That's how you keep winning—and still have somewhere worth coming home to when the lights go down.

Who's your most important customer at home? And do they *feel* like it?

When was the last time you invested the same energy into that relationship that you give to your biggest client?

Every climb demands a sacrifice.

What are you *willing* to trade to reach your next summit in time, comfort, ego, sleep?

And what are you *never* trading again?

Carl Lenocker

The older I get, the more I realize something nobody tells you in your twenties:

Winning isn't the finish line. Winning is just another mile marker. Another hotel room. Another night where the lights go down and you ask yourself the only question that really matters:

What was all of this for?

You can master the steakhouse arena. You can carry the quota, close the deal, shake the hands, and wear the miles like medals. You can do everything it takes to win without losing the people who matter most.

But eventually—whether it's at 2 a.m. in a Marriott, or somewhere over Kansas in seat 8A, or standing at your kitchen counter waiting for the coffee to brew—the noise dies down long enough for the truth to get through:

Success isn't the story. *Meaning* is.

The road teaches you how to win. But reflection teaches you *why* you wanted to win in the first place.

And once you've felt the cost of winning in your bones, you start looking beyond the next quarter. Beyond the next steakhouse. Beyond the next badge or title or performance review.

You start looking backward—toward the people who built you... and forward—toward the people you're building for.

You start asking questions that don't have dashboards or KPIs:

Have I honored where I came from? Have I built something my kids can stand on? Would the people who raised me recognize the man I've become? Would they be proud?

Those are the questions that started rising in me as I approached fifty—not as regrets, but as reminders.

Because the truth is, none of this—*none* of it—makes sense without the past that forged you.

The late nights. The hard miles. The parents who tried their best with what they had. The grit you inherited. The tenderness you learned. The mistakes you carried. The fire you built from nothing.

That's where the next chapter begins.

Not with a deal. Not with a trophy. Not in a boardroom or a hotel bar.

But with time. With memory. With the people who gave you your first compass, even if they never got to follow theirs all the way home.

Before you can honor your life by designing the future… you have to honor the lives that designed you. And that's where we go now.

Into the chapter that reminds us that every mile, every moment, every sacrifice…

wasn't just part of the story.

It *was* the story.

It was everything.

CONCLUSION
IT WAS EVERYTHING

Because honoring the past is how you build the future.

My fiftieth birthday is coming fast, and I find myself thinking a lot about time, not in years or quarters anymore, but in moments. Moments that built me. Moments that tested me. Moments that shaped who I became.

When I turn fifty, I'll be doing it on a luxury yacht in Cabo San Lucas, anchored somewhere off Medano Beach with family and close friends. I'm going to be doing it in the best shape of my life, and while celebrating some pretty significant financial milestones, and all of it seems like a huge reach from where my story began.

When I look at my life today, I'm proud, not because it's perfect, but because it's intentional.

I didn't build a great life to outrun my past. I built it to honor it.

To show my kids that no matter where you start, you can design a life that means something.

You can break patterns but still love the people who lived inside them. You can build systems that last, without losing your soul.

They Weren't Broken; They Were Brave

It's easy to assume that motivation like mine comes from pain, from wanting to escape, from being angry at what was missing. But that's only partially correct.

My parents weren't broken. They were brave.

My dad had grit in his hands and faith in his work. He knew he wasn't a perfect person, but he kept trying, kept moving forward, all the way until the end. He taught me that strength isn't about never breaking, it's about getting back up every time life knocks you down and tightening your grip on the wheel.

He taught me that if you're going to do something, you do it right, even when nobody's watching. Cut corners once, and it'll come back to haunt you. That's how he lived. If that meant tarping a load when there was only a 5 percent chance of rain, then so be it.

His lessons on showing up, even when you don't feel like it, still stay with me today. The world's full of people who start strong and fade fast. He wasn't one of them. He believed a man's reputation wasn't built in a single victory, but in the hundred small days no one ever applauds.

My mom had a dreamer's heart: creative, sensitive, and far more complex than most people ever understood. Her life was tragic and beautiful all in the same breath. She fought demons her whole life. Depression. Addiction. The kind of pain that doesn't announce itself: It just quietly eats away at the edges of joy until there's not much left.

She never got the help she needed. And when she died, a light went out that had been growing dimmer for many years. I still put in the work, daily, on not blaming myself for not being able to save her. For a long time, I thought her story ended in tragedy. But now I'm starting to see it differently.

She was love in its rawest form: unfiltered, generous, and totally flawed. She taught me empathy. She taught me presence. She taught me that strength isn't always loud; sometimes it's the act of simply waking up early and cleaning your house. Trying again, to get through one more day.

And though she never saw the full picture of what my life became, I carry her in everything I build. Every chapter. Every plan. Every word. She is the soft heart beneath the systems.

Driving East

I thought about all of this on a road trip with my daughter Scarlet just after she graduated college. We were driving east to Florida, her new life waiting on the other side of the map.

Four days of highway, playlists, and quiet stretches that felt like time travel. Her in the passenger seat, me at the wheel, the same formation I once shared with my dad decades ago.

But this time, I was the one steering; I was the dad now. As the miles rolled beneath me, the road turned into a reel of my life, playing frame by frame in my mind. Every mile hummed like a memory: the wins, the wrecks, the near-misses that shaped who I'd become. The road had taken a lot from me, but it had given me something greater: the stories that would outlive me.

Somewhere between the asphalt and the sky, I found myself thinking about my family—the road that raised me, the sacrifices that built my foundation, the quiet grit that got me here. And in that still stretch of highway, it hit me: This was the life my parents had both wanted for me.

The Truck on the Highway

Outside Tallahassee, I saw a rig ahead with my dad's old company logo on the side. This was unusual because there are only a couple hundred operating in North America at any given moment. Same font. Same color. Same rattle in the engine.

I glanced instinctively toward the driver's window, half-expecting to see him there, hand on the wheel, eyes forward, navigating another long stretch of American road.

A few hours later, that same truck pulled into a truck stop beside us. The Jake brake groaned, the air brakes hissed, and I felt something catch in my throat. I exhaled deeply.

Scarlet noticed.

"Dad, are you okay? What is it?" she asked.

I nodded. "Nothing, it was nothing."

But my voice cracked.

It was everything.

Because the truth is, in that moment, I saw my whole life, every mile, every mistake, every lesson, condensed into the sound of that engine.

It wasn't sadness. It was gratitude.

For the man who taught me to work hard and to stick with it, when times got tough.

For the woman who taught me to feel deeply and to be ready to meet the Queen at any moment.

And for the chance to give both of their legacies a happy ending.

Would They Be Proud?

If my dad could see me now, I think he'd be proud. Not because I made money or built a career, but because I kept my word. I never became the man guarding the executive restroom. I didn't cut corners. I stayed true to my roots. I left the door open for others. I made sure the job got done right.

And if my mom could see me now, I think she'd smile, that soft, tired smile I remember from childhood, and she'd know that her love didn't die with her. It lives on in the way I show up for my wife, my kids, and my clients.

And that ten-year-old boy sitting between them, looking out the window of that old Freightliner?

He'd be proud too.

Because the man he became didn't just survive the road, he paved one for others to follow.

It Was Everything

When Scarlet and I finally crossed into Florida, the sun was setting.

She was quiet, staring out the window, taking in the start of her next chapter. Scared, I'm sure, like when Mom landed, pregnant with me at SFO in 1976, ready to start a new life in a foreign land.

I smiled, not because I was ready to let her go, but because I knew she was ready to fly.

The systems were in place. The lessons were written. The legacy was secure.

And as we drove into the golden light, I thought about my parents, the courage, the chaos, the love, the loss, and I whispered to myself, "It was everything."

Because it was.

Every hard mile. Every sleepless night. Every risk and reward.

It all added up to this moment.

A life that means something.

A family that's strong.

A story worth passing down.

STOP AND REFLECT

If you've read this far, you already know: Success planning isn't about control.

It's about care.

It's about designing a life that honors where you came from, protects who you love, and gives them the tools to keep climbing long after you're gone.

Build the systems.

Leave the door open.

Be The One who changes everything.

And one day, when your kids are driving down life's highway toward their own new life, they'll glance at the sky, think of you, and whisper softly, "It was everything."

You stuck with me through every mile, every memory, every ghost on the highway.

So if you're still here… alright then.

Here's your bonus chapter. Don't say I didn't warn you.

BONUS CHAPTER
SO YOU WANT TO BREAK INTO THE ENTERPRISE SOFTWARE GAME

If you made it all the way to this point, after my childhood trauma, the airports, the steak dinners, the hotel mishaps, and the hangovers, and you *still* want to break into the enterprise software game...

Then God help you.

But also, welcome. You might actually have what it takes.

Most people read about this life and tap out halfway through. The travel, the pressure, the politics; it's too much. But a few of you... you're wired for it. You see the art in it. You read this book and thought, "Yeah, I could do that."

So, this one's for you: the brave, the foolish, the ones who want to climb into the ring.

Lesson One: Nobody Hands You a Badge

This game doesn't have an application portal.

Nobody's waiting to hire you because you love tech or work well with people.

You've got to fight your way in one rejection, one unanswered email, one awkward networking call at a time.

The people who make it here? They earn it. They claw their way through the noise, through layoffs, through recruiters who never call back.

You don't stumble into enterprise software, you decide to be here.

Lesson Two: Go Get Your Scars Early

If you're young, or hell, even if you're not, go get yourself a job that teaches you pain.

An SDR or BDR role is perfect.

That's where you learn the rhythm of rejection and the beauty of not giving a damn about it. You'll dial, get hung up on, ignored, ghosted, and lied to and still find a way to hit quota.

You'll learn how to sell yourself before you ever sell software.

That's the muscle you'll use for the rest of your career in every deal, every customer call, every internal battle.

Both my daughters are in those trenches right now, making calls and taking punches. It's not glamorous, but it's real. And nothing builds grit like a thousand tiny noes.

Lesson Three: Get Close to the Customer

At some point, you've got to learn what it feels like to stand in front of a customer when things go wrong.

That's where this business separates the storytellers from the survivors.

Go work for a partner or reseller, somewhere you'll have to talk to real people, fix real problems, and eat real shit sandwiches. Learn how to calm down an angry CIO (chief information officer), explain technical nonsense in plain English, and survive an escalation call when everyone's losing their minds.

You can't lead customers if you've never been in the fire with them. And believe me, there will be fire.

Lesson Four: Climb Smart, Not Fast

When you finally break in, resist the urge to sprint to the top. You want to land somewhere around 3,000–5,000 employees, a company that's big enough to have process but small enough to notice when you're killing it.

The dream is to find a company that's either pre-IPO or recently public. Why? Because the real game isn't salary, it's equity.

Your goal is to get that first block of Restricted Stock Units (RSUs), then stack stock refreshers year after year. You do that for four or five years, and you'll look around one day and realize you've built something solid: wealth, reputation, and leverage.

You don't need to be the smartest. You just need to stay in the chair long enough for compounding to kick in.

Lesson Five: Build a Reputation That Outlives Your Business Card

Enterprise software is a revolving door with layoffs, mergers, new logos, new leaders. The only thing that sticks is your name.

You have to build your brand inside and outside your company. Write posts. Comment on other people's. Speak up. Be seen as someone who knows their craft and helps others without being a jerk about it.

You want to be the name that people think of when an opportunity opens up. Visibility isn't vanity, it's insurance.

Lesson Six: Be Cool Under Fire

You'll learn quickly that this game isn't for the faint of heart.

You'll have customers yelling, systems crashing, and execs breathing down your neck, sometimes all before 9 a.m.

Your job is to stay calm. To lead. To be the one person in the room who doesn't panic when everyone else does.

That's how you earn trust. And trust, not titles, is what gets you paid.

Lesson Seven: Lower the Ladder

If you've made it, even just a little, reach back. Take the call from the hungry kid who wants your advice. Help the laid-off engineer trying to pivot into CS.

I take those calls every week, and I'll never stop. Because that's how this industry stays human—by people helping people climb.

Lower the ladder. Someone did it for you.

Final Lesson: Know What You're Signing Up For

If you really want in—I mean really—understand what you're signing up for. This isn't a nine-to-five. It's a lifestyle.

You'll wake up in cities you barely remember landing in, chasing renewal deadlines, watching stock prices swing, and living on coffee and adrenaline. You'll get addicted to the wins and be haunted by the losses.

But you'll also meet some of the best people you'll ever know. You'll build friendships in airports, in Slack threads, and over bourbon in dim hotel bars. You'll grow tougher, wiser, and more self-aware than you thought possible.

Carl Lenocker

And one day, when someone asks you how to break into enterprise software…

you'll smile, shake your head, and say, "Careful what you wish for. But if you're still serious, pull up a chair."

ABOUT THE AUTHOR

Carl Lenocker is one of the world's top Customer Success Executives, known for his no-BS leadership style, his steakhouse-table strategy sessions, and his ability to turn customers into lifelong partners.

From growing up broke in a Texas motel to becoming a Silicon Valley multi-millionaire, Carl's journey embodies the core philosophy behind *Success Plan for Life*: Design your success with intention—before someone else designs it for you.

Carl has spent over two decades helping customers, teams, and individuals build success plans that align purpose with performance. His writing blends street-level experience, business leadership, and emotional intelligence to teach others how to turn ambition into action.

When he's not working with clients or speaking on stage, you'll find him on the road—exploring new cities, mentoring rising professionals, or contemplating his next move in an airline lounge somewhere.

Carl welcomes booking inquiries for speaking engagements, coaching sessions, or consulting services.

Connect with Carl:

Website: www.SuccessPlanForLife.com

LinkedIn: www.RockstarCSM.com

Instagram: @SuccessPlanForLife

Email: Carl@RockstarCSM.com

www.ingramcontent.com/pod-product-compliance
Lightning Source LLC
LaVergne TN
LVHW051044080426
835508LV00019B/1704